Self-Employment
From Dream to Reality!

By Linda D. Gilkerson
&
Theresia M. Paauwe

Self-Employment
From Dream to Reality!

©1998 by JIST Works

Published by JIST Works, Inc.
720 N. Park Avenue
Indianapolis, IN 46202-3490
Phone: 317-264-3720 Fax: 317-264-3709 E-mail: jistworks@aol.com
World Wide Web Address: http://www.jist.com

See the back of this book for additional JIST titles and ordering information.
Quantity discounts are available.

Interior Design by Debbie Berman

Printed in the United States of America

2 3 4 5 6 7 8   02 01 00 99 98

ISBN 1-56370-443-9

Contents

The World of Business

*O*wning a business has always been part of the American Dream, but today more people than ever are considering self-employment. Maybe you're thinking of starting a business because you've been "downsized." Perhaps you have the technology to work from home. Or maybe you just looked at the quality of your life and decided you need a change.

In this chapter, we'll look at the reasons people give for going into business for themselves. We'll explore the personality traits of successful business owners, review the main reasons that businesses fail, and look at how to avoid many of these pitfalls. And we'll show you why *planning* your business is not only time well spent but the *only* way to create a healthy and profitable venture.

In the space below, list all your answers to this question: Why do you want to own a business?

_____

_____

_____

_____

Of course, there are no right or wrong answers to this question. But your reasons are important because they will be the measure of your success. For instance, let's say one of the reasons you list is spending more time with your children. If, a year after starting your business, you find you are working more hours than ever before and actually seeing your children less, is your business a success? Or perhaps you want to own a business to make more money. If, after several years, you are still stretching to pay your bills, is your business a success?

One of the best things about self-employment is that *you* get to define what success means. And your definition is shaped by the reasons you want to go into business.

Before we go any further, let's define two terms we'll use throughout this book:

☛ **Entrepreneur:** One who manages, organizes, and assumes the risk of a business or enterprise.

☛ **Microenterprise:** A very small business operating from a home, storefront, or office that employs five or fewer employees (and often only one!).

Do You Have What It Takes?

Successful entrepreneurs come from all different backgrounds and experiences. Age, gender, marital status, and education levels do not seem to be significant factors for success. But there are some skills that successful entrepreneurs share. As you look through the following list, determine the areas in which you excel, and identify the areas in which you need work.

◆ What skills and experiences do you have that are key to the success of the business you want to own? Successful entrepreneurs have skills to sell.

_____

_____

_____

_____

◆ Are you responsible? Do you do what you say you will do, when you say you will do it? Can people count on you? Entrepreneurs are responsible.

_____

_____

_____

_____

◆ Do you have good social skills? Do you say what you mean? Do you listen well? Entrepreneurs must be able to sell themselves.

_____

_____

_____

◆ Are your financial and personal situations stable?

_____

_____

_____

◆ Are you optimistic? Entrepreneurs think positively.

_____

_____

_____

◆ Do you have a strong motivation to achieve? Entrepreneurs are doers.

_____

_____

_____

◆ Are you a hard worker? Do you work hard for others? Entrepreneurs often work more than 40 hours per week.

_____

_____

_____

◆ Do you have problem-solving skills? Do you enjoy solving problems? Entrepreneurs are problem solvers.

_____

_____

_____

◆ Are you independent? Entrepreneurs are leaders, not followers.

_____

_____

_____

◆ Are you afraid of making decisions? Do you have a take-charge attitude? Entrepreneurs make all of the decisions for their businesses.

_____

_____

_____

◆ Do you accept responsibility? Entrepreneurs accept responsibility for their own businesses.

_____

_____

_____

Following is a list of personality traits that are common to successful entrepreneurs. How many of them do you possess?

- Motivation to achieve

- Capacity for continued hard work

- Nonconformity

- Strong leadership ability

- Street smarts

- Responsibility

- Optimistic outlook

There also are personality traits that are not conducive to successful entrepreneurship, including these:

- Compulsive in gambling

- High risk taking

- Impulsive or inclined to "shoot from the hip"

Finally, there are factors that are less important—they seem to make no difference to one's capacity for success:

- Age

- Gender

- Marital status

- Education level

Business Failure

We've all heard the bad news. Here are some common statistics that scare many people away from self-employment:

- One in three new businesses fail within six months.

- Three of four start-ups shut down within five years.

- Nine out of ten companies operating today will eventually fail.

Scary statistics indeed. But recent studies suggest there is much more to know about business successes and failures. A 1988 study by Babson College and the Small Business Administration found the failure rate of small business start-ups to be significantly lower than previously thought.[1] And many of the "failures" are more accurately called "career changes," as no money was lost and the closure of the company was voluntary.

David Birch (1987) puts the success rate even higher, alleging that 75 percent of small businesses survive their first few years.[2]

Additionally, a 1993 study by the Entrepreneurship Program at the New Jersey Institute of Technology found that no more than 18 percent of business start-ups fail during their first eight years; 28 percent survive the first eight years with their original owners; 26 percent survive the first eight years with a change of ownership; and 28 percent of businesses voluntarily terminate operations without losses to creditors.

So, although some businesses do fail, the chances for success are better than you might think.

Why Do Businesses Fail?

Let's look at some of the reasons that businesses fail. Knowing some of the pitfalls *before* you start your business can help you avoid them. We will address most of these problems in this workbook.

◆ **Owner's personality not suited to running a business.** Business owners who are reluctant to make decisions or who lack self-discipline have a greater chance of failing. Businesses run on relationships. Customers need to trust the owner so they will be comfortable doing business with him or her. A business owner who has difficulty getting along with people will be at a disadvantage.

◆ **Poor choice of business opportunity.** Some fields in the marketplace are saturated. For example, it seems you can't drive a city block without seeing a pizza place, an instant print shop, or a video store. Lots of competition means you must have something terrific to offer customers that your competitors don't. These are risky business ventures, simply because there are so many of them.

◆ **Inadequate start-up capital.** Many businesses begin without enough money in reserve. Chances are, it will take longer than you expect to find customers and to generate enough income to support the business. On the other hand, if you make good decisions when spending your start-up capital, you may actually need less than you originally estimate.

In the beginning, invest your cash in people and things that will result in sales— not in "flash." Forget the fancy office, the car phone, and other toys *unless they are absolutely necessary to make sales.* Sometimes, leasing or renting equipment can save you money during the start-up phase. Ask yourself this question *before* you buy anything: How will this expenditure result in sales?

◆ **Poor selection of location.** If you are locating your business outside your home, choose your spot based on where your customers live, shop, or visit. Do not base this decision on proximity to your home. Don't take a space simply because it happens to be available on the first day you're looking. Try to leave your emotions out of the decision. This is especially important for retail businesses. When you're looking at a potential spot, ask yourself this: Will this location result in sales?

◆ **Lack of knowledge about attracting customers.** You must have a plan to get customers to try your product or service. You can't simply offer lower prices than your competitors and be successful. Remember, consumers are creatures of habit. They must have a reason to change their spending habits.

◆ **Failure to seek professional advice.** It is critical that you seek the advice of an accountant and, depending on your business, an attorney. Save yourself grief by finding and hiring an accountant in the beginning. Your business also may require other professionals. You probably have expertise in the business you have chosen but, chances are, you are not an authority on every aspect of your business.

◆ **Poor choice of legal form.** You need to understand the different legal forms of business so you can make an informed decision about which is best for you. Later, we will discuss sole proprietorships, partnerships, and different types of corporations. There are many factors to consider, and taxes are an important one. So this may be a decision you want to discuss with your accountant and attorney.

◆ **Insufficient experience in product or service.** Some people dive into a business without understanding how that particular industry works. As a result, they may set up a pricing structure that will not allow them to make a profit. Or they might produce an inferior product or service. Successful business owners either have experience in the industry or take the time to research it thoroughly *before* taking the plunge.

◆ **Insufficient planning and investigation.** Many people spend more time planning their vacations than they do planning their careers. There will always be surprises, but if you take the time to plan, fewer issues are left to chance. Planning will accomplish one of two things: (1) You will decide your business idea won't work or you are not ready; or (2) you will be convinced that you have a good idea that can work, and you will be comfortable with the risk of self-employment.

> *Remember, a business owner who fails to plan, plans to fail!*

Planning Your Business Is Critical

Many people float aimlessly through life, taking its ups and downs as they come, just getting by, living from day to day. If they become successful, or even comfortable, it's more by accident than by plan. This approach rarely works for a business.

Proper planning allows you to try out your business on paper, with no financial risk. Your plan is your road map: It tells you where you should be at any given time, when you are succeeding, when you need to make adjustments, even when it's time to get out.

It's impossible to know everything you need to before going into business. There's so much information, it is staggering. But you should figure out *what* you need to know before starting the business, and then plan to continue learning.

Learn to plan and plan to learn!

Your Best Bet Is a Business Plan

If you have spent any time researching self-employment, you probably have encountered *the business plan*. And if you are like most people, the more you read about business plans, the more confused you became. There are several different outlines to choose from, all with different sections. Some outlines use questions, some use big business words. And the main thing many people draw from these "helps" is that a business plan is very complicated. But it doesn't have to be. A business plan can be a simple, effective tool for planning, financing, and growing your business.

Before we discuss what a business plan should look like, let's look at why a business plan is critical to your success:

◆ **A business plan can give you the confidence to start your business, or it can help you realize that your business idea is not a good one.** Before you make the final decision, you need to think through the answers to many questions about your product or service, your customers, your pricing, your marketing, and your potential cash flow. Your business plan gives you a process for answering those questions in an organized and logical way.

◆ **After you have started your business, you can refer back to your business plan to keep you focused on the next task.** A business plan is never finished. It changes as circumstances in your business change. But it can be used as a guide to build and manage a successful business.

◆ **A business plan is a small business's best tool for raising money.** Most financial institutions will insist on a business plan to evaluate your idea. Your business plan gives the loan officer information about you and your idea, and allows him or her to evaluate your business's credit-worthiness.

◆ **A business plan can be a marketing tool.** As you write your business plan, you will have a clearer picture of your business. This will help you explain what services or products your business will provide, who your customers will be, and what your goals are for the business. Have your employees read your business plan so they understand what you want to accomplish.

You will find an outline of a business plan on the following pages. As you read it, don't get hung up on the information you don't have. This workbook will lead you, step-by-step, through the writing of your own business plan.

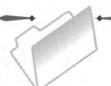

Business Plan Outline

1. Introduction

Title page

Name of business and your name.

Your address and telephone number.

Write the words "Business Plan" on the title page.

Table of contents

Pages should be numbered.

General description of the business

Describe the business you want to start.

What services or products will you offer?

Where will you locate?

Explain why you choose this business.

What are the skills and experiences you bring to the business?

What are your goals for the business?

What is your action plan to achieve these goals?

2. Marketing

Product or service description

What is your product/service?

What is the demand for your product/service?

Market description

Who is your customer? How do you know? Describe any market research by industry experts or any research you have done. Is this a fad or a trend? How will your market grow or change over the next few years?

Competition

List your competitors and identify their strengths and weaknesses.

Compare prices, product quality, etc.

What advantages will your business have over the competition?

Selling strategy

How will you sell your product or service?

What is your pricing strategy?

What advertising will you do?

What promotions will you do?

How will your product or service be delivered?

3. Organization

Quality control

How will you ensure the quality of your products or services?

Legal structure
In what legal form will you do business? Why is this best for you? If more than one person is in the business, include agreements.

Insurance
What insurance will your business carry?

Management
How will your business be managed on a day-to-day basis?
Who will be responsible for monthly financial reports?
How will management change in the future?
How will your business records be maintained?

Advisors
Who is your accountant?
Who is your attorney?
Who are the people you can turn to for good advice?

Other issues
Discuss any other issues pertinent to your business.

4. *Financial plan*
What equipment or supplies will you need?
What are your resources?
What financing will you need?

Cash-flow projections
Monthly: use "best guess," "high side," and "low side" numbers.

Operating budget
Provide a monthly budget for the first year.
Provide "what-if" statements.
If you are using your business plan to request a loan, you should also include the following:
> Supporting material
> Brochures, business cards, summary of market research, references from people who know you or the business.

Purpose and amount of the loan
An exact dollar amount you want to borrow for the business, and how the money will be used.

Explanation of your personal credit
If you have had any credit problems, acknowledge them and explain how the problem has been resolved.

Summing Up

Ready to get started? After reading though the business plan outline, you may think there is too much information to know. But this workbook will help you gather the necessary information and make decisions based on that information. Learning is like building with blocks. What you learn at first determines which questions you need to answer next. Let's start by examining your choice of businesses.

Notes

1. *The Wall Street Journal* (May 20, 1988): 27.

2. David Birch, *Job Creation in America: How Our Smallest Companies Put the Most People to Work* (New York: Free Press, 1987).

Defining Your Dream

Some people are very clear about what business they want to start. But it's perfectly acceptable to decide first that you want to start a business, then read, listen, and search for the business that would work for you. You should begin the process by thinking about who you are, what you enjoy doing, and how you really want to spend your time.

After you decide what kind of business you want to start, take time to daydream and develop a clear mental image of your business. Imagine yourself doing the business. This is the first step in communicating your idea to others. Write a brief description of your business, and practice saying it. Select a name for your business; this will make it feel like a reality.

In this chapter, you'll identify the business you want to start and your support people for this new adventure. It is important to know who those people are *before* you need them. To get started, read through, think about, then answer the following questions:

◆ What are your gifts and talents? A gift is anything you do very well or something that comes easily to you.

_____

_____

_____

_____

◆ What are your passions? Does your life have a mission? Is there something you feel so strongly about that you want to spend your time convincing others of its worth?

_____

_____

_____

_____

◆ What have you read or heard that interests you? Spend some time reading and learning about what businesses others are starting. Be open to opportunities.

_____

_____

_____

_____

_____

_____

Where to Find Business Opportunities

☛ The public library

☛ Entrepreneurial magazines

☛ Newspapers

☛ Friends or acquaintances

☛ The *Yellow Pages*

◆ What are your personal goals? Be sure to consider your lifestyle. It's important to select a business that satisfies you and involves work you love and do well.

_____

_____

_____

_____

◆ List the business possibilities you are considering. List the advantages and disadvantages of each business. Consider start-up costs, hours, the type of work, and any other factors you can think of.

_____

_____

_____

_____

Business Possibilities	Advantages	Disadvantages
_____	_____	_____
_____	_____	_____
_____	_____	_____
_____	_____	_____
_____	_____	_____
_____	_____	_____

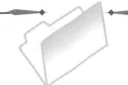

Narrow Your Choices

Talk to people in the selected business.

Read about those businesses. Try to find real numbers about the businesses.

Ask your accountant or your banker.

Share your ideas with family and friends, and be ready to listen to their reactions.

Make your final decision.

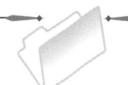

25 Top Home-Based Businesses in 1995

- Auto detailing
- Coffee house
- Consulting
- Desktop publishing
- Event-planning service
- Financial aid service
- Gift basket service
- Herb farming
- Home computer operator
- Home health agency
- Home inspection service
- Information broker
- Import/Export business guide
- Mail order business
- Medical claims processing
- Micro-brewery
- Operation of "900" number for profit
- Property tax consultant
- Restaurant
- Secretarial/Word processing
- Seminar promoting
- Travel agency
- Utility/Telephone bill auditing
- Vending machine business
- Wedding planning service

Every successful business starts as a daydream in the owner's mind. But most people get so caught up in daily living they don't take time to be quiet and dream. The time you spend imagining yourself making your product or service and actually running your business is time well spent. Some people have such strong, vivid images of their businesses, they are practically compelled to start them. So get comfortable, close your eyes, and "see" your business. Take time to dream every day until your thoughts begin to seem possible and real. Use the following questions to get started; and when you have the answers, write them in.

◆ What is my business dream?

_____

_____

_____

_____

_____

◆ Where is my business place and what are my equipment needs?

_____

_____

_____

_____

_____

◆ Who are my customers?

_____

_____

_____

_____

_____

◆ What type of work am I doing?

_____

_____

_____

_____

_____

In later chapters, we'll discuss how to determine if your business idea will work. But, at this beginning stage, the best thing you can do is talk about your idea. Be prepared to listen carefully to people's reactions to your idea. Try not to take comments personally; instead, use the feedback to determine if your business idea should be discarded or if you should continue your investigation. And don't be discouraged if you discard several business possibilities before finding one that seems possible. Be prepared to take your time and think through each idea. To investigate a business, you must learn and listen; fortunately, both are inexpensive activities.

Spend time thinking through how you will explain your business idea to others. If you want someone to listen to your idea and react to it, you must be very clear in what you say. Practice your description often, so when you have an opportunity, you can describe your business dream clearly in just one sentence.

Communication Exercise

Read through the dialogue below. Imagine the patient friend's reaction to the business starter's rambling answer to the question, "What is your new business?"

Business Starter: "I'm going to start a new business!"

Patient Friend: "Oh, really? What is your new business?"

Business Starter: "Well, **you know how**, have you ever, you know, thought about, um, starting to do something different in your life? You know like when your job is a drag, and your boss is a jerk, and you aren't making any money, so you decide to start your own business, but, you know, think about how **difficult it would be if you decided that you wanted to go into business for yourself but you had no idea**, absolutely no idea. I mean how would you? You know? How would you know, even, **where to begin?** Huh? Well, you wouldn't because, how many times before have you ever gone into business for yourself? Really! Think about it, it would be a totally foreign experience. Okay! So **even if you went to the library and read books about it, most of that material is written**, and I mean, I really know this is true, it's written **in business language, which most people don't understand.** So, my idea would be, I mean, if people thought it would work, I mean … I don't know, so, I'd have to ask a lot of people if they thought it would work, but if a lot of people thought it might work, I could do this … well, I think I could do this … but anyway, **my business** idea **would** be to **provide training to those people who have no idea how to start a business of their own.** After all, I've had my own business before, so I have some experience in this, and I have a friend who has had a couple of businesses, and she could help me. **And my training would be in plain English, using words everyone can understand**, because, after all, I mean, I know I'm a good communicator. I mean, don't you feel bad for people who really want to quit their jobs and would if they could, but they just don't know how to … they just don't know where to begin to, **and**, well anyway, **I would base the training around writing a business plan**, and we could talk about, oh!—and this would be really cool!—experiences *other* people have had starting *their* own businesses. And I would provide, you know, resource materials about how to name your business, and I could teach people about marketing and financial stuff, and, you know, all kinds of stuff that people would need to know, but don't know, you know, about starting their own business. You know? What d'ya think?"

Impatient Friend: "Have you met that new guy in accounting?"

Now, go through the dialogue again, this time reading only the bold sections of the business starter's answer. What is the friend's reaction now? It's important to practice describing your business as concisely and precisely as possible.

Here is a good practice exercise. Suppose you are being interviewed by a TV reporter, and you have 15 seconds to respond to this question: "What business are you in?"

_____

_____

_____

_____

Make a list of people with whom you want to share your business idea. Jot down their reactions.

_____

_____

_____

_____

_____

What's in a Name?

Everyone knows how important a name can be, whether you're talking about a baby or a new business. We all know businesses with great names (and businesses with so-so names). Be prepared to spend time finding the right name for your business. As you gather information about your business, keep tossing names around in your head. Be sure to write them down. A word you jot down today may sound great with another word you think of next week. Take time to select the best name for your business because, whatever you choose, you'll have to live with it. Make sure the name you select meets most of these criteria:

◆ It quickly identifies what you do

◆ It stands out from the competition

◆ It's easy to remember

◆ It's easy to spell and pronounce

◆ It's neither too short nor too long

First, **brainstorm** a long list of words that describe what you want your business to reflect. Think of adjectives, feelings, features, and images you have about the business. You can use a name that tells what the business does, that communicates the primary benefit of your product or service, or that describes the main activity of your business. Or you can simply make up a name.

Next, **piece the words together**. How do they sound together? Do they convey the image you want for your business? **Remember your customers**. Will they remember the name? **Share the best names with friends**. Listen to their reactions. Don't panic if you don't have the perfect name as you begin planning your business. As you gather information and your dream becomes more real to you, you'll find the right name.

Identify Your Support Team

The decision to start a new business is yours to make. But it's important to identify people who will be supportive *before* you begin your business. Although financial support is obviously helpful, you should also think about who in your life will give you emotional support, objective critiques, realistic views, and new ideas. You need people around you who believe in your dream and your ability to realize it. Having people offer enthusiastic support, nonjudgmental suggestions, and consistent encouragement greatly increases your likelihood of success.

So, who are the supportive people in your life?

_____

_____

_____

Starting a business is a major life change, and, even though the change is positive, *it will be stressful*. You also are creating major changes for your family, and their fears and concerns may make it difficult for them to be supportive right now. Don't be discouraged: Later, these same family members will be able to celebrate your successes with you. In the meantime, look for other sources of support among your network of extended family, friends, and business associates.

Summing Up

The first step in developing a clear mental image of your business is to consider your gifts, talents, and interests. We hope you are convinced of the importance of your daydreams. Communicate your business idea to people and identify your friends or family who will be supportive. Now, let's look at the next step to make our dreams come true: how will we be able to finance our dreams?

Financing the Dream

*F*inancing your business can be a difficult task. Before you approach a lender or investor, it's important to understand the lending process and to be well prepared.

In this chapter, you'll learn the language of finance and read about the "Four Ps" and "Five Cs" of credit. You'll also look at your credit options, and what you need to do to finance your dream.

A Look at Your Business

1. Do you personally have enough money to finance your business dream?   Yes _____   No _____

   If you checked no, answer the questions below.

2. How much money (in cash, equipment, and inventory) can you invest in your business?

   _____

3. Do family or friends have money they are willing to invest in your business?   Yes _____   No _____

   If so, how much?

   _____

4. If you and your family and friends cannot invest enough, how much money do you need to borrow to start a new business or to maintain your existing business?

   _____

5. Write down how you would use invested or borrowed money in your business:

Amount	Purpose
$ _____	_____
$ _____	_____
$ _____	_____
$ _____	_____
$ _____	_____
$ _____	_____
$ _____	_____

6. Where can you go to borrow this money?

_____

Financing 101

The dream of being self-employed is an exciting one, but a common obstacle to realizing that dream is the lack of money. Even if you succeed in starting a business, it often is difficult to get a loan to maintain or grow it.

Before you seek money for your business dream, you should understand the basics of financing. In this section, we'll look at what a lender considers when reviewing a loan request, some common financial terms, how to identify essential business needs, how to create a financial plan, and why it's important to develop a relationship with your lender. We'll also review the loan application process, personal credit reports, and what you can expect if your loan request is approved.

The Risky Start-Up

Financing a business start-up is the riskiest loan a lender can make. A start-up business doesn't exist, so the owner cannot demonstrate its capacity to make a profit (and repay the loan). Even if the entrepreneur has significant experience producing the same product or service, being a successful entrepreneur requires a different set of skills.

For example, entrepreneurs must market and sell their products or services. They must manage cash flow daily, keep accurate records, understand financial reports, and use them to make informed decisions. They must set prices that are not too high or too low. Entrepreneurs must relate well to customers, employees, suppliers, and creditors. In time, successful entrepreneurs develop strong business management skills; but often, mistakes are made along the way. The magnitude of those mistakes can mean the difference between success and failure.

The business owner stands to benefit the most from (and has the most control over) a business success. Because of this, the owner is expected to assume the most risk when starting a business. Start-up businesses usually are financed through the personal resources of the business owner: savings, investments, equity in a home, and loans or investments from family and friends.

Sometimes, the entrepreneur must find a lender willing to finance the start-up. That lender is taking a chance on the unproved abilities of the entrepreneur, often a person not well-known to the lender. It is in the best interests of the entrepreneur to develop an honest relationship with the lender. The entrepreneur must provide sufficient, convincing information that the business start-up represents a worthy risk. The lender has to believe in the business idea and trust the entrepreneur. That trust must be earned, and building trust takes time.

The Existing Business

Once a business owner has gathered enough resources to start a small business, is it any easier to get credit? The answer depends on a number of factors: the owner's relationship with the lender, the financial strength of the business, the way the owner manages the business, the borrower's ability to repay the loan, and an alternative method of repaying the loan if the business isn't as profitable as the owner projected.

Sometimes, a business owner approaches a lender only when the business is in financial crisis. The owner then is desperately seeking cash as a short-term solution to a significant problem, often with no long-range plans to keep the problem from reoccurring. This owner is unlikely to get a loan. Lenders prefer to develop long-term relationships with business owners who take the time—and have the ability—to manage their businesses well.

A borrower needs a clear idea of how much money the business needs and how the money will be used to maintain the business. If the business owner cannot explain these things clearly to the lender, the loan request likely will be denied. A lender is looking for a clear plan that explains how the money being borrowed will be invested to strengthen the business: in other words, how the loan will help the business generate the additional income required to repay the loan.

It is important to prove that the business is borrowing enough money, but not too much money. For example, a business may need money to buy equipment that will significantly increase its capacity to produce a product. With proper planning, increased production should result in increased sales. If the owner borrows too little, the equipment cannot be purchased. The borrowed money might be spent on operating costs until the funds are depleted. In the end, the business is left with no increase in sales and a debt it cannot repay.

Likewise, a business that borrows too much money may not increase its sales enough to generate the cash required to repay the loan. The key to determining how much money your business should borrow is proper planning.

Before turning to the steps of financing a business, let's look at some common financial terms.

The Language of Finance

◆ **Capital** is the money, equipment, or other major contribution invested to start a business. This usually is put into the business in a fairly permanent form, such as major equipment or land. Capital typically is not recovered until a business is sold. Capital can come from two sources: owners and lenders.

◆ **Equity capital** is money the business owner or other people invest. Equity capital carries with it a share of ownership and, usually, a share in the profits.

◆ **Debt capital** is money an owner borrows to start a business. This money must be repaid to the lender with interest.

◆ **Equity (or net worth)** is what remains when everything a company owes (its liabilities) is subtracted from everything a company owns (its assets). Equity can be greater than or less than the amount of capital invested in the business.

◆ **Collateral** is something of value the borrower owns and is willing to pledge as a secondary method of repayment if he or she fails to repay the loan in cash. The lender "secures" (lays claim to) the collateral at the time the loan is made, so that no other lender can secure the same collateral during the life of the loan.

◆ **A loan** is money that is borrowed and must be repaid, usually under specified terms and conditions. Most banks and investors require the business owner to provide 35 to 40 percent of the capital before they will approve a loan. There are three common types of loans:

   ◈ **Short-term loans** provide money for short periods of time, usually 30 to 90 days. The original amount you borrow and must repay is called the *principal*. The fee charged for borrowing the money is called *interest*. In a short-term note, the money is used for the term of the note; then principal plus interest is repaid all at once.

   ◈ **A line of credit** is an approved amount of money a borrower can access as needed. The repayment on a line of credit is established at the beginning of the loan. Repayment terms are flexible and may include monthly, interest-only payments and quarterly or annual principal repayments.

   ◈ **Long-term loans** often are used to buy real estate or equipment, and the purchased item is secured for collateral. (That is, the lender retains ownership of the real estate or the equipment until the loan is paid back.) Long-term loans have repayment terms of more than 12 months. Monthly payments are made, with a portion applied to interest and the remainder applied to the principal.

◆ **Working capital** is the amount of money available to pay short-term expenses. It's like a cushion to meet unexpected or out-of-the-ordinary expenses. A working capital loan can help a start-up business pay operating expenses for a short time as the business becomes self-sustaining. To get this kind of loan, a financial plan must show a business's ability to reach sustainability in a reasonable period of time.

Getting a Loan

Identify Your Needs

The first step in financing your business is to identify your needs. Don't think in terms of dollars; think in terms of what your business needs. Do you need to buy equipment or inventory? Are you looking for a way to test your market?

Once you have a list of your needs, examine it carefully and ask yourself this question: Is everything on the list essential? To determine this, identify those items that will generate money for your business and those that won't. Say, for example, you own an alterations business, and you need a new sewing machine. Clearly, the sewing machine will generate income for your business: It's essential. A cellular phone might be convenient and a new desk might be nice, but they won't generate income for your business: They are not essential.

You must use your judgment to separate essential and nonessential items. You might be able to operate your business inexpensively from your home. But if your customers expect your business to be located in an office or storefront, then renting space might be the only way to succeed.

Once you have listed your essential needs, it's time to calculate their cost. You must request a loan amount that finances essential items and makes sense for your business. Don't begin the financing process with a dollar amount in mind. And don't base your request on how much you think you can borrow.

Develop a Financial Plan

The next step is creating a financial plan. Your plan will show the loan money coming into your business and your "essential needs" purchases being made. It will show money coming in from sales and money going out to pay expenses. Of course, it will show your business repaying the loan over a specific period of time. There are a few things a lender will want to see in your plan:

◆ **The projections must seem reasonable.** If you are financing a start-up business and you project high sales from the first day, your projections may not be realistic. In most businesses, sales start slowly and increase over time.

◆ **If your business will have seasonal fluctuations, these should be reflected in the plan.** A business that sells Christmas trees may have sales in November and December, and none the rest of the year.

◆ **Finally, your operating expenses and the salary you take out must relate to the scale of your business.**

In Exercise #1, you will review two financial plans prepared for Dave's Lawn-Mowing Service. Try to think like a loan officer. Which plan seems like the best bet for your financial institution?

Exercise #1

Dave wants to borrow $2,000 to start a lawn-mowing service. He plans to start the business in January, operate the business part-time, and have no employees. Review Dave's first financial plan below, then answer the questions that follow.

Dave's Lawn-Mowing Service

Six-Month Financial Plan #1
Loan Request: $2,000
Business Start-Up Date: January 1

Cash In	Start-Up	Jan	Feb	Mar	Apr	May	Jun	Total
Loan proceeds	$2,000							$2,000
Lawn-mowing income		$1,500	$1,500	$1,500	$1,500	$1,500	$1,500	$9,000
Total Cash In	$2,000	$1,500	$1,500	$1,500	$1,500	$1,500	$1,500	$11,000

Cash Out								
Lawn mower	$1,500							$1,500
Gas & oil for mower		$350	$350	$350	$350	$350	$350	$2,100
Truck expenses		$250	$250	$250	$250	$250	$250	$1,500
Advertising		$100	$100	$100	$100	$100	$100	$600
Insurance		$25	$25	$25	$25	$25	$25	$150
Loan payments		$0	$175	$175	$175	$175	$175	$875
Owner's salary	$500	$775	$600	$600	$600	$600	$600	$4,275
Total Cash Out	$2,000	$1,500	$1,500	$1,500	$1,500	$1,500	$1,500	$11,000

Remaining Cash Balance	$0	$0	$0	$0	$0	$0	$0	$0

1. Does Dave's plan seem realistic?   Yes _____   No _____   Why?

_____

_____

2. How does Dave plan to use the loan money? _____

3. Does Dave include a plan to repay the loan?   Yes _____   No _____

4. Do Dave's sales projections seem reasonable? Yes _____   No _____
   Is his salary reasonable?   Yes _____   No _____
   Do his expenses seem reasonable?   Yes _____   No _____

5. How could Dave improve this financial plan? _____

_____

6. Based on this financial plan, would you loan Dave the $2,000 he is requesting?
   Yes _____   No _____

Dave has revised his business idea. Notice that in his revised plan, Dave has decided to wait until April 1 to start his new business. Review Dave's revised plan below, then answer the questions that follow.

Dave's Lawn-Mowing Service

Six-Month Financial Plan #2
Loan Request: $2,000
Business Start-Up Date: April 1

Cash In	Start-Up	Apr	May	Jun	Jul	Aug	Sep	Total
Loan proceeds	$2,000							$2,000
Lawn-mowing income		$350	$450	$550	$650	$800	$800	$3,600
Total Cash In	$2,000	$350	$450	$550	$650	$800	$800	$5,600

Cash Out								
Lawn mower	$1,500							$1,500
Gas & oil for mower		$35	$45	$55	$65	$80	$80	$360
Truck expenses		$53	$67	$83	$97	$120	$120	$540
Advertising		$50	$50	$50	$50	$50	$25	$275
Insurance		$25	$25	$25	$25	$25	$25	$150
Loan payments		$175	$175	$175	$175	$175	$175	$1,050
Owner's salary	$0	$50	$100	$150	$200	$325	$400	1,225
Total Cash Out	$1,500	$388	$462	$538	$612	$775	$825	$5,100

Remaining Cash Balance	$500	$462	$450	$462	$500	$525	$500	$500

1. Does this plan seem more reasonable than the first?   Yes _____   No _____
    Why? _____

2. How does Dave plan to use the loan money?

3. Does Dave include a plan to repay the loan?   Yes _____   No _____

4. Do Dave's sales projections seem reasonable?   Yes _____   No _____
    Is his salary reasonable?   Yes _____   No _____
    Do his expenses seem reasonable?   Yes _____   No _____

5. How could Dave improve this financial plan? _____
    _____

6. Based on this financial plan, would you loan Dave the $2,000 he is requesting?
    Yes _____   No _____

The Application Process

Loan application requirements vary among lenders. You probably will be required to submit a business plan (or at least an executive summary) that describes the products or services you will sell, short- and long-term goals for your business, information about you and your management staff, your marketing strategy, and financial information.

When you are using your business plan to get financing, you should include a specific financing request. The financing request, or *use of funds* statement, is simply a breakdown of how you propose to use the loan. The use of funds statement should be as detailed as possible, including equipment, model numbers, descriptions, and prices. Include catalogs or brochures describing the equipment you want to buy. Remember that your use of funds statement must be supported by the financial plan you submit. Here is an example of a use of funds statement:

Use of Funds Statement

Equipment:	Lanford Laser Printer Model EP5 with 1,000-sheet paper-feeder cassette (see brochure attached)	$1,000
Advertising:	*Town Crier Newspaper*, 1/2" display ads for 4 weeks; Radio advertising 30-second spots (see details attached)	$500
Working Capital		$1,000
Total Loan Request		**$2,500**

Your lender probably has a loan application packet. Pick up the packet and take it home with you. Fill it out neatly and completely. Don't forget to attach any additional information the lender requests, such as personal financial statements or tax returns. *If you have questions, ask them.* If you or your business have issues that may be of concern to your lender, don't try to hide them: Bring them up when you make your loan request and address them honestly.

Get to Know Your Lender

While you are in the early stages of identifying your needs and creating your financial plan, begin establishing a relationship with your lender. Stop in and say hello. Introduce yourself. Tell the lender you are in the planning stages of financing a business. Don't take a lot of his or her time talking about your business idea before you're ready to make your loan request. Simply let the lender know who you are, and that you intend to approach him or her when you are ready.

The Four Ps of Finance

☞ **Preparation:** Be thorough when you prepare your business plan, and be prepared when you approach lenders and investors.

☞ **Presentation:** You must be ready and able to sell yourself and your business to others. Practice with friends before you approach lenders and investors.

☞ **Positive attitude:** You must project confidence in yourself and in your business. A positive attitude comes from thorough preparation, practice, and a strong belief in your ability to succeed.

☞ **Persistence:** This might be the most important ingredient in getting financing. Prepare to be turned down several times before you succeed. If you are turned down, ask yourself: How can I make this work? What can I change to get the financing I need? Finding money is not always easy, but it is possible!

It's also a good idea to do your personal banking at the institution where you plan to request your loan. If you have a separate business checking account, some banks will even require that you have it there. And don't do your banking at the drive-through window. Go into the office, stop by the loan officer's desk, and say hello.

Remember, business is about relationships. People do business with people they know and like. Whether yours is a start-up or an existing business, begin a relationship with the lender well before you need a loan. After all, you'll be asking the lender to share a financial risk with you, and your working relationship will last a long time. So let the loan officer get to know you. Be a familiar face!

Personal Credit

Someone has been watching you! Each time you've signed for a car loan, used a credit card, or taken out a mortgage, the activity has been reported to a credit bureau. If you have a history of making late payments, it shows up on your personal credit report. If you have failed to repay a loan as promised, had a court judgment against you, had any tax liens filed against you, or filed personal bankruptcy within the last 10 years, it shows up on your credit report. But there's good news, as well: If you have made your payments on time, repaid your debts as promised, and have a track record of being a reliable credit risk, that shows up on your credit report, too!

Most applications for personal credit require you to sign a form that allows the creditor to obtain a copy of your personal credit report. Likewise, when you request financing for your business, lenders will require you to sign forms that allow them to obtain your personal credit report. Your personal credit is a major consideration, even when you are applying for a business loan. (Your lender is taking a risk on you as well as your business.) Your credit report tells a story about you, and you should know what the story is before you apply for a loan.

Order your own credit report at least once a year, and check it for accuracy. Sometimes credit bureaus make mistakes, and other people's credit transactions can show up on your report. You can ask a credit bureau to correct errors on your report by filing the appropriate paperwork. Be prepared to prove your claims. If you have difficulty getting a credit bureau to remove an item from your report, you can at least have them note that the entry is in dispute. If you are (or were) married, and you and your spouse have (or had) joint accounts, each of your credit reports will include those accounts.

Your report may show a poor credit history at a time when you experienced some hardship, such as a divorce or a medical catastrophe. You probably can address this on your credit report. Most credit bureaus allow you to submit a short narrative explaining the circumstances of poor or questionable credit. This narrative will appear when a creditor requests a copy of your credit history. Many lenders are willing to take hardships into consideration when reviewing your credit. You must address these issues with your lenders: Tell them what they will find *before* they find it, and be honest.

If your report reflects a recent or current period of poor or no repayment, your lender will look for indications that you are trying to rebuild your credit. There are several ways to do this. One of the best is to get help from a nonprofit, consumer credit counseling agency. These agencies help you get copies of your credit history, correct reporting errors, and establish a plan to rebuild your credit.

You've Been Approved! Now What?

If your loan request is approved, your lender may write a commitment letter that outlines the terms and conditions of the loan. Lenders are required by law to state clearly the interest rate charged on a loan: This is called *Annual Percentage Rate (APR)*. Your lender will schedule a loan closing, at which time you will sign the documents required by the lender and receive your loan proceeds. Typical loan documents include these:

◆ **A promissory note.** When you sign this note, you promise to repay the loan under the specified terms.

◆ **A security agreement.** By signing this, you give the lender a secured interest in the collateral you have pledged.

◆ **A personal guaranty.** Lenders usually require the owner(s) of a business to personally guarantee the loan. This means that if the business is unable to repay the loan for any reason, the owner(s) agree to assume personal responsibility for repayment.

Read all the loan documents carefully, and ask questions about anything you don't understand, before you sign anything.

Your lender may charge closing fees to help cover the administrative costs of the loan. Ask about closing fees before the closing. Fees can be paid by the borrower at the closing, deducted from the loan proceeds, or added to the balance of the loan.

An Interest in You!

Lenders are businesses, and they cover their operating and administrative expenses by charging interest on loans. Interest is the fee the borrower pays in exchange for access to credit. Interest typically is charged according to an annual percentage rate (APR): If your annual interest rate is 12 percent, you will be charged 1 percent interest (one-twelfth) on the balance of your loan each month. Below is an amortization schedule that shows the principal and interest breakdown of each monthly payment. Your lender can explain how interest and principal is calculated on your loan.

Amortization Schedule

Loan Date:	**26-Jan-97**
Amount:	**$2,000.00**
Interest Rate:	**12.00%**
Term:	**24**
Payment Amount:	**$94.15**

Payment #	Due Date	Beg Bal	Amt Paid	Interest	Principal	Ending Bal
1	01-Mar-97	$2,000.00	$94.15	$20.00	$74.15	$1,925.85
2	01-Apr-97	$1,925.85	$94.15	$19.26	$74.89	$1,850.96
3	01-May-97	$1,850.96	$94.15	$18.51	$75.64	$1,775.32
4	01-Jun-97	$1,775.32	$94.15	$17.75	$76.39	$1,698.93
5	01-Jul-97	$1,698.93	$94.15	$16.99	$77.16	$1,621.77
6	01-Aug-97	$1,621.77	$94.15	$16.22	$77.93	$1,543.84
7	01-Sep-97	$1,543.84	$94.15	$15.44	$78.71	$1,465.13
8	01-Oct-97	$1,465.13	$94.15	$14.65	$79.50	$1,385.63
9	01-Nov-97	$1,385.63	$94.15	$13.86	$80.29	$1,305.34
10	01-Dec-97	$1,305.34	$94.15	$13.05	$81.09	$1,224.25
11	01-Jan-98	$1,224.25	$94.15	$12.24	$81.90	$1,142.35
12	01-Feb-98	$1,142.35	$94.15	$11.42	$82.72	$1,059.63
13	01-Mar-98	$1,059.63	$94.15	$10.60	$83.55	$976.08
14	01-Apr-98	$967.08	$94.15	$9.76	$84.39	$891.69
15	01-May-98	$891.69	$94.15	$8.92	$85.23	$806.46
16	01-Jun-98	$806.46	$94.15	$8.06	$86.08	$720.38
17	01-Jul-98	$720.38	$94.15	$7.20	$86.94	$633.44
18	01-Aug-98	$633.44	$94.15	$6.33	$87.81	$545.63
19	01-Sep-98	$545.63	$94.15	$5.46	$88.69	$456.94
20	01-Oct-98	$456.94	$94.15	$4.57	$89.58	$367.36
21	01-Nov-98	$367.36	$94.15	$3.67	$90.47	$276.89
22	01-Dec-98	$276.89	$94.15	$2.77	$91.38	$185.51
23	01-Jan-99	$185.51	$94.15	$1.86	$92.29	$93.22
24	01-Feb-99	$93.22	$94.15	$0.93	$93.22	($0.00)
	Total:	**$2,000.00**	**$2,259.53**	**$259.53**	**$2,000.00**	**($0.00)**

* Ending Bal = Beg Bal – Principal

Summing Up

Your business plan is your primary tool for getting financing for your business. The business plan gives important facts about your business, including these:

◆ Long- and short-term goals

◆ A description of the products and services you will offer

◆ The background and experience of the owner and management staff

◆ Your marketing strategy

◆ The business's financial plan

◆ The financial history (if any) of the business

◆ The financing needs of the business

◆ How a loan will be used to start or strengthen the business

Finally, as you prepare your loan request, keep in mind what lenders look for in a borrower—the Five Cs of Lending.

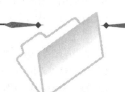

The Five Cs of Lending

☛ **Character**: The owner's personal integrity

☛ **Capacity**: The company's financial strength and ability to repay its debt

☛ **Capital**: How much debt the company has compared to its equity

☛ **Collateral**: A secondary source of repayment

☛ **Conditions**: The conditions of the economy and the industry

The Goal Train

*F*or some people, life goes around and around, like a train on a circular track. They work, pay bills, and deal with family and friends day after day, year after year, around and around. In this chapter, we'll look at how you can throw the switch on the tracks, so you can go new places and accomplish new things.

On Your Mark, Get Set, Goal!

Most people would agree that setting goals is an important step in fulfilling dreams. Yet only 5 percent of Americans actually write down their life goals and monitor them. The process of setting goals is not complicated, but it does require you to be honest with yourself and to do some serious thinking about what you really want to achieve.

Keep in mind that successful people *do* set goals; and they use these goals to make decisions and keep themselves focused. Since setting goals is an important step in achieving what you want from life, let's go through the process of naming your goals, then using them to stay focused on what you really want from life.

In Chapter 2, we discussed how every business begins with a dream. In this chapter we'll look at the eight steps to taking control of our lives and sending our "train of life" along different tracks.

Let's take a brief look at the eight steps before we go into detail:

1. **Know yourself.** Knowing who you are gives you a sense of direction. Take time to inventory your strengths and weaknesses.

2. **Define your values.** Your values are what you believe in and what you would like to represent. They determine how you treat people, the relationships you seek, and your ideas of right and wrong. Values are your fundamental convictions.

3. **Establish your goals.** Write goal statements that are achievable and measurable.

4. **Create an action plan.** Base your plan on the information you have about yourself, your values, and your goals. List the steps you need to take and the resources (money and time) required to accomplish your goals. Prioritize the steps. Ask yourself a couple of questions: Are these goals realistic? Do you have the necessary resources available to implement your plan?

5. **Examine your motivation.** Positive motivation excites, energizes, and generates excellence. Motivation is a key ingredient of success.

> *A goal is a dream with a deadline!*

6. **Learn discipline.** Successful people do not succumb to procrastination or temporary setbacks. They overcome obstacles with an inner strength: discipline. You can learn to be disciplined. The more disciplined you become, the more control you will have over your life.

7. **Be flexible.** Be ready to constantly reevaluate yourself, your values, your goals, and your action plan. Be ready to modify your strategies when change occurs, because it will.

8. **Reach an outcome.** The outcome is the destination of your journey. When you arrive, take time to evaluate your trip. Did you accomplish what you set out to accomplish? What did you learn along the way? Get ready to set your next goals.

In the following pages, we'll look at each of these steps in more detail.

Know Yourself

Who are you? Explain yourself in terms of your attitudes and your self-image. What do others think of you? What do you do well? What tasks are you uncomfortable doing? What are your weaknesses? Try not to define yourself in terms of what you own or in terms of "shoulds." And don't define yourself in terms of the roles you play (mother, husband, daughter, etc.).

In the space below, write a short description of who you are. Be honest. This inventory may be uncomfortable, but it is necessary if you want to improve yourself or make decisions about your new business.

_____

_____

_____

Define Your Values

Have you ever dreamed for months about going on a great vacation, then had that vacation be a miserable experience? The same thing can happen if the decisions in your life are not based on sound values. The outcome may leave you feeling dissatisfied and empty.

Values—also called principles, ideals, purposes, beliefs, and convictions—are your most important, fundamental beliefs.

Suppose your goal was to win a race, but in order to win, you tripped your opponent. Would the outcome leave you feeling triumphant? Probably not.

How you play is based on your values, and this holds true in business, too.

◆ What values do you want to instill in your children?

_____

_____

_____

◆ What three values would you want people to identify with you?

_____

_____

_____

Establish Your Goals

Any farmer can tell you: When you plow a field, you must keep your eyes fixed on one point on the horizon. Without that fixed point, your row will meander all over the field. The same is true in life. If you don't keep a specific target in sight, you'll wander off course.

Your goals must be specific. It's not enough to simply say you want to be happy, or successful, or wealthy, or to travel. Your goals also should be measurable; they should have a time frame as well as an intended result. If you don't clearly define both a time and an intended result, how will you know when you've reached the goal?

> *Remember, your goals and business objectives must be in agreement with your basic values.*

Goals should answer the following questions:

◆ Where am I going?

◆ How am I going to get there?

◆ How much will it cost me to get there?

◆ How long will it take me to get there?

◆ How will I know when I have arrived?

Your goals should be challenging, but realistic. Set goals you think you can reach: It's better to up your goals later than to set them so high that you give up. Setting goals that are unreasonable is self-defeating; they'll only keep you from succeeding.

Visualize your goals. When you begin to "see" a dream, you can make it happen. Once you've visualized them, write your goals down, keeping in mind that a list of goals is more than a list of chores.

Reward yourself when you reach your goal. Reward yourself for the great effort you put in, even if the goal did not turn out completely as expected.

Create an Action Plan

There's an old Chinese proverb that applies here: The journey of 10,000 miles starts with a single step. Focusing only on the end result doesn't get you where you need to be today or tomorrow. It may only overwhelm you.

You must determine what steps you need to take *today* to reach your outcome. Planning brings the future into the present, so you can do something about it. What needs to be done to make your dream a reality? Where do you start? What strategy will work best? What resources will give you the outcome you want?

At the end of this chapter you will find goal activity pages on which to record your goals, the steps to reach them, your target dates, the person responsible, the money and time required, and the results.

When you have finished reading, write your goals, list the steps, prioritize them, and *begin*! Don't wait until the conditions are perfect. Expect problems, and tackle each one as soon as you encounter it.

If you are afraid of taking action, don't look at all the steps ahead of you. Concentrate on one step at a time. Focus just on what is required to complete that single step. Then do it!

Examine Your Motivation

To be successful in your own business, you must make things happen. You are the only one who can build the bridge between thinking about your goals and accomplishing them. Self-motivation is the driving force behind high achievement. It's the inner desire that keeps you always moving forward in spite of discouragement, mistakes, and setbacks. There are several "steps" to self-motivation, including these:

◆ **Believe in yourself.** Make success and happiness part of your self-image.

◆ **Think only positive thoughts.**

◆ **Welcome challenges.**

- ◆ **Be flexible to change.**

- ◆ **Take pride in your achievement.**

- ◆ **Set goals that are stimulating, challenging, and achievable.**

- ◆ **Overcome fear.** Fear is the opposite of desire. It creates stress, panic, and anxiety, and defeats plans and goals. To overcome fear, you must understand where it's coming from. Then take action; *action cures fear*.

- ◆ **Start now.** Don't wait until you have all the information or the circumstances are perfect. Begin now. Get in motion as soon as possible. As your momentum builds, so will your motivation.

- ◆ **Focus on the rewards.** Visualize the rewards of success in your mind as clearly and vividly as you can.

Learn Discipline

Being disciplined means sticking to an action plan even when there are other things you'd rather do. It is hard work. It takes guts. It means staying focused and practicing better work habits.

Being disciplined means taking responsibility for yourself. Many people are quite good at blaming others for their own shortcomings. It's easy to blame outside forces for failure. But if you are going to be a successful entrepreneur, you must stop making excuses and take charge of your own life and your own success.

You may need to start small. Take control of your day *today*. This is the first step in taking control of your success.

Be Flexible

Change is constant; you cannot avoid it. Try to see change as an opportunity instead of as a problem. Change is growth: It can improve your life if you let it. Accept change in your life as normal and positive. Don't just stand there, change!

Reach an Outcome

Whatever the outcome of your goal, hold it in high regard. Focus on what you did right instead of what you did wrong. Then set another goal.

If these ideas are new to you, read them again until you begin to believe them. Then, practice setting goals. Soon, you'll be convinced that it's the best way to take control of your life and your business.

Three Scenarios

Meet Gail, Jerry, and Daryl. Each has a new business venture. Read the descriptions of their business ideas and the goals they have set for themselves. What do you predict will be the outcome for each? Why?

> *Remember, your business goals must mesh with your personal goals and values if you are going to succeed!*

How to Make an American Quilt

Gail plans to make quilts at home and sell them on consignment through craft boutiques, home decorating stores, and the colonial village tourist site outside of town. She has received a loan of $1,200 to buy a cutting table, cutting tools, and an old sewing machine. Four stores have agreed to take a total of 10 quilts on consignment, and she has a good list of additional stores to contact.

Gail plans to spend about 25 hours a week sewing, and 5 hours a week making new contacts. Each quilt takes about 15 hours to make.

Gail has set several goals for the next six months:

◆ To purchase a table, cutting tools, and supplies within the next month

◆ To start sewing by the end of the first month

◆ To average 1½ quilts per week, and to deliver the 10 quilts that have already been accepted for consignment within the first two months

◆ To sell 8 quilts a month

◆ At the end of six months, to reevaluate goals and decide if there is enough business to invite a friend to work with her part-time

Painting Himself into a Corner?

Jerry has been painting houses to earn money on the side, helping out a buddy with a painting business. Now Jerry has been laid off from his factory job, and he's decided to start painting full-time. His buddy needs help sometimes, but he prefers to work alone when he can handle it. So Jerry has decided to start his own business. Jerry has no experience in soliciting jobs; he's just worked on them.

Jerry figures, to make it work, he has to meet these goals:

◆ Get an $8,000 loan to buy a used truck and the ladders and equipment he'll need before he can take any jobs

◆ Paint 50 hours a week, and do publicity 10 hours a week

◆ Find a minimum of three jobs per month for the first three months

◆ By the end of three months, increase from three jobs to nine jobs per month, and hire a helper

Jerry figures he can collect unemployment for the first three months. But once his unemployment runs out, he'll have to double his business. To handle that much work, he'll have to hire a helper, which means more expense. So he really needs to triple his business to make enough money to cover his bills and living expenses.

Hot Stuff or a Hot Spot?

Daryl makes a mean chili. His buddies have been telling him for years that he should sell the stuff. He has a job, which he'll keep, but he's decided to start his own business on the side. He's going to call it *Hot Stuff*.

Daryl got the idea for his business while he was at a concert in a downtown park. There were several food concessions there selling mediocre food at high prices. Daryl figures he's got a better food product. There must be a way to make money charging the kind of prices he saw at the concert.

Practice Writing Effective Goals

Effective goals should be realistic, measurable, and state a target date. Rewrite the following statements so each becomes an effective goal.

1. Increase sales by $3,000. _____

2. Triple total sales within three months. _____

3. Hire new employees within a year. _____

4. Visit several other businesses to get new ideas. _____

5. Grow from one site to three before Christmas. _____

6. Improve publicity this year. _____

7. Buy a new pickup by the time I start taking jobs. _____

    _____

8. Within the next two months, visit community workers who could tell families about my childcare service. _____

9. Move workspace out of my home. _____

10. Set aside $500 to hire an artist to design packaging. _____

    _____

Daryl's got enough money put away to buy a small cart with a warming unit for about $800. He figures the first time there's a big concert downtown, he'll cook up a big batch of his best chili and head for the park. Hey, what does he have to lose?

Write Your Own Goals

In the exercise that follows, you will write your own goals, both personal and business. State your goal, the action plan to reach the goal, the target date, the person responsible, the money and time required, and the results. After you write all your goals and action steps, prioritize them, and *begin*.

Goal/Action Plan

My ultimate goal is:_____

_____

_____

This is my ultimate target date: _____

Here are the steps I will take to reach my goal, along with the target date for each:

1. _____

2. _____

3. _____

4. _____

The person responsible for each step is:

1. _____

2. _____

3. _____

4. _____

The money and time requirements are:_____

_____

_____

Here are the results: _____

_____

_____

_____

Goal/Action Plan

My ultimate goal is:_____

_____

_____

This is my ultimate target date: _____

Here are the steps I will take to reach my goal, along with the target date for each:

1. _____

2. _____

3. _____

4. _____

The person responsible for each step is:

1. _____

2. _____

3. _____

4. _____

The money and time requirements are: _____

Here are the results: _____

_____

_____

Goal/Action Plan

My ultimate goal is:_____

_____

_____

This is my ultimate target date: _____

_____

Here are the steps I will take to reach my goal, along with the target date for each:

1. _____

2. _____

3. _____

4. _____

The person responsible for each step is:

1. _____

2. _____

3. _____

4. _____

The money and time requirements are: _____

_____

_____

Here are the results: _____

_____

_____

Summing Up

Remember, successful people set goals. So, if you want to go to new places and accomplish new things, begin to know your strengths and weaknesses. Take time to examine your values so you can establish goals that will draw you where you want to go. Don't forget to create an Action Plan that lists the steps and the time and money required to accomplish each step. In the next chapter, we will discuss how to price your products and services to make a profit.

5

Pricing Your Products and Services

Proper pricing can mean the difference between success and failure in your business. When businesses don't take the time to examine their price structures, they may find (often too late) they have not priced their products or services properly.

Underpricing can cause a business to fail; if products are drastically underpriced, the business loses money every time a sale is made. Overpricing can cause sales to disappear altogether, as customers buy from lower-priced competitors.

In this chapter, you'll learn about pricing products and services. You'll also learn to perform a break-even analysis to determine if your price structure is sound.

1. Write down why you think proper pricing is important.

    _____

    _____

    _____

    _____

    _____

2. Why do you believe business owners under- or overprice products or services?

    _____

    _____

    _____

    _____

    _____

3. List some of the consequences of underpricing.

_____

_____

_____

4. Why do you think business owners are unaware that their products are not properly priced?

_____

_____

_____

_____

A business should have two aims in determining its pricing system: (1) to price its products or services competitively and (2) to ensure that all business expenses can be paid and a profit earned, given a reasonable level of sales. In order to make this happen, the business owner needs to answer the following questions:

◆ What prices are appropriate for my market?

◆ What are my business expenses?

◆ What are reasonable sales goals for my business?

In the following sections, we'll look at how you can answer each of these questions accurately, so you can ensure proper pricing for your business.

What Price Is Right?

The real price of a product or service is no more than the customer is willing to pay. Finding out how much your customers are willing to pay requires some research on your part. Below are several sources of information on pricing. Use as many of them as you can to determine what prices are appropriate for your market.

Customer Surveys

One way to determine pricing is to survey your potential customers. This is possible only if you can easily identify and locate your potential customers, which, for some businesses, is difficult. It also may be a challenge to get an honest answer to the question, "How much would you be willing to pay for this?" Some businesses mail surveys to their target customers, and some survey individuals in public places.

Shopping Your Competition

Another way to find out what the market will bear is to "shop" the competition. If your competitors operate from retail stores, a quick trip to their shops allows you to see what they charge for similar products and services, and whether they appear to be making sales. You can make phone calls to determine hourly rates commonly charged by service industry competitors. This way, you not only find out what your competitors charge, you also get a good feel for their level of customer service. Shopping your competition allows you to experience whether your competitors are respectful to their customers, answer and return phone calls promptly, and are knowledgeable about their industry.

Market Research Sales

Selling your goods or services at a marketplace or fair—or temporarily subleasing a small space in an existing shop—is an effective way to determine appropriate pricing, as well as help you determine if your business idea is feasible. This approach also gives you hands-on experience at operating your business. In order to use this approach, you will need a small supply of inventory. You should make certain you are not required to rent booth or floor space in a long-term lease. Remember, this is just an exercise in market research to help you determine how to price your products.

While you operate your temporary business, listen to what your customers tell you. If customers continually comment on how low your prices are, you may have some room to raise them. On the other hand, if your products create interest but no sales, you might consider lowering your prices.

What Are Your Expenses?

In order to operate a successful business, the pricing structure must take into account all of the expenses of running the business. Expenses must be identified and divided into two categories: cost of goods sold and fixed expenses.

Cost of Goods Sold

The direct expenses of creating your product or service are called the *cost of goods sold (COGS)*. If your business sells wooden toys that are handcrafted and painted, then the wood, the paint, and the time it takes to make the toys are all COGS. If your business sells beaded jewelry, then all of the materials (beads, thread, glue, clasps, pins, etc.) plus the cost of labor (the time it takes to make each piece of jewelry) are the COGS. If you provide a service, such as a secretarial service, the COGS might include paper and file folders, plus the cost of the labor. In a cleaning business, the COGS might include cleaning supplies, transportation costs for cleaning crews, and labor.

Fixed Expenses

Some expenses exist whether or not a business has any sales. These are called *fixed expenses*. Examples of typical fixed expenses include rent, insurance, utilities, legal and accounting costs, and advertising. These expenses sometimes are referred to as *overhead expenses*. Fixed expenses do not substantially increase or decrease with changes in sales volume. Because of this, fixed expenses are easy to identify.

The Break-Even Analysis

Once your COGS and your fixed expenses have been identified, you can perform a *break-even analysis*. This tells you how many products or services you must sell at a given price in order to cover the expenses of your business. The break-even point is the point at which adequate sales are made to cover your business expenses, but before a profit is earned. It's important to perform this analysis, because it allows you to determine if your price structure is sound. This will also give you minimal sales goals for your business.

Just a Few More Terms …

Before we actually perform a break-even analysis, let's define a few terms.

◆ **Gross income** is the amount of income a business earns, before expenses are considered.

◆ **Gross profit** is what remains when you subtract the cost of goods sold from the gross income. It is from the gross profit that fixed expenses are paid.

◆ **Net profit** is what remains when you subtract the fixed expenses from the gross profit.

Typically, this is how the information is put together:

ABC Widgets & Gadgets

Income

Sales/Widgets	$500.00
Sales/Gadgets	$400.00
Gross Income	$900.00

Cost of Goods Sold

Materials	$250.00
Labor	$350.00
Total COGS	$600.00
Gross Profit	$300.00

Fixed Expenses

Rent	$100.00
Utilities	$ 35.00
Total Fixed Expenses	$135.00
Net Profit	**$165.00**

When Will You Break Even?

In order for your business to succeed, you must have sufficient gross income so that after you subtract your cost of goods sold, there is enough gross profit to pay all of your fixed expenses. The break-even point defines the actual number of products or services you must sell at a certain price in order to achieve this. A new business performs a break-even analysis after assuming the following three things:

1. **Gross income (or price) per product or service.** At first, this number is an educated guess based on what you learned about the marketplace. The break-even analysis will confirm whether or not this price is sufficient.

2. **Cost of goods sold per product or service.** You find this number by researching the cost of creating the product or service.

3. **Fixed expenses of the business.** This information comes from researching the cost of operating the business.

Once this information is gathered, a break-even analysis is performed using the following two-part formula:

Gross income − cost of goods sold = gross profit

Fixed expenses ÷ gross profit = break-even point

For example, if we assume the following about a widget business:

Gross income per widget =	$9
Cost of goods sold per widget =	$4
Fixed expenses per month =	$1,000

then, we can perform the break-even analysis as follows:

Gross income	$9
− cost of goods sold	− $4
= gross profit	$5
Fixed expenses	$1,000
÷ gross profit	÷ $5
= break-even point	200

This business must sell 200 widgets per month at $9 per widget to break even.

Now go through the following example to see how Sarah Sue performs a break-even analysis for her new business.

Sarah Sue's Scenario

All of Sarah Sue's friends rave about her sandwiches (she makes them with her secret sandwich sauce). With a great deal of encouragement from her family and friends, Sarah Sue is thinking about opening her own sandwich shop. At this point, she is in the information-gathering stage.

Sarah Sue has learned that a local deli owner is about to retire, and she has talked with him about renting his storefront. (This will cost her $450 per month.) Sarah Sue also got information about the costs of utilities for the storefront (about $150 per month), telephone (about $100 per month), and business insurance ($25 per month). Sarah Sue examined her personal situation and made a determination about how much money she needs to earn in order meet her financial obligations ($1,000 per month).

Armed with this information, Sarah Sue came up with the following list of fixed expenses for Sarah Sue's Sandwich Shop:

Next, Sarah Sue must calculate the cost of goods sold for her sandwiches. Since the ingredients for the sandwiches will vary by order, Sarah Sue decides to start with what she believes will be her most popular sandwich: turkey and Swiss cheese on whole wheat (known as the *Swiss Gobbler*). She calculates the cost of making this sandwich with everything on it, since this will represent the highest COGS. Having received a price sheet from her food supplier, this is what Sarah Sue comes up with:

Fixed Expenses

Rent	$450
Utilities	$150
Telephone	$100
Business insurance	$25
Owner's salary	$1,000
Miscellaneous	$50
Total fixed expenses:	$1,775

Supplier Price Sheet and Labor Costs	Sarah Estimates	Ingredients per *Swiss Gobbler*	COGS *Swiss Gobbler*
Turkey $3.00/lb.	10 slices/lb.	2 slices	$ .60
Bread $ .50/loaf	32 slices/loaf	2 slices	$ .03
Swiss cheese $3.00/lb.	10 slices/lb.	2 slices	$ .60
Mayonnaise $2.00/jar	32 ounces/jar	1 ounce	$ .06
Mustard $1.00/jar	32 ounces/jar	1 ounce	$ .03
Tomatoes $ .12 ea.	8 slices/tomato	2 slices	$ .03
Lettuce $ .60/head	30 leaves/head	2 leaves	$ .04
Secret sauce $3.00/jar	32 ounces/jar	1 ounce	$ .09
Wax paper $ .03/sheet	precut sheets	1 sheet	$ .03
Labor @ $5.00/hr.	20 sandwiches/hr.	3 minutes	$ .25
Total COGS:			**$ 1.76**

Sarah Sue has determined that it will cost her $1.76 to create her most popular sandwich. She has shopped the competition and surveyed her friends, and she believes that a fair price for this sandwich will be $3.50. Given these assumptions, Sarah Sue calculates the following:

$$\text{Gross income} - \text{COGS} = \text{gross profit}$$
$$\$3.50 - \$1.76 = \$1.74$$

$$\text{Fixed expenses} \div \text{gross profit} = \text{break-even point}$$
$$\$1,775.00 \div \$1.74 = 1,020$$

Sarah Sue knows she will have to sell 1,020 *Swiss Gobblers* (or similarly priced sandwiches) each month to break even. To break the calculation down further, if Sarah Sue is open for business six days a week, or about 25 days each month, she will need to sell about 41 sandwiches per day to break even. Now, she can ask herself if this seems like a reasonable goal.

$$1{,}020 \text{ sandwiches} \div 25 \text{ days a month} = 40.8 \text{ sandwiches a day}$$

Man Does Not Live by *Swiss Gobblers* Alone

Sarah Sue did a break-even analysis for one sandwich, the *Swiss Gobbler*, but what if she sells many kinds of sandwiches? And what if she wants to sell other items, such as beverages, French fries, and chips? How do we perform a break-even analysis on a variety of products? When a business offers a variety of products for sale, that variety is known as the *product mix*.

To determine pricing for your business's product mix, perform a break-even analysis on each product you will sell, as Sarah Sue did for the *Swiss Gobbler*. Once these analyses are done, you can estimate how many of each product you will sell in a given period of time. Multiply the gross profit for each item by the number you think you will sell. Then add the total gross profits together. Does this total gross profit equal or come close to your fixed expenses? If not, keep playing with the numbers sold until you get a product mix that does come close. When you have estimates you believe are reasonable and adequate to cover your fixed expenses, you will have the break-even point for your product mix.

When you are doing this, make some assumptions that make sense for your business. For example, Sarah Sue knows that she has to sell 1,020 *Swiss Gobblers* to break even. She believes all of her sandwiches will be similarly priced, but she also wants to sell other products, such as French fries and beverages. She must price these products so that she makes a gross profit on each. She may not sell a beverage each time she sells a sandwich, but she may sell one with 90 percent of her sandwich sales. She may not sell French fries with each sandwich, but she may sell them with 75 percent of her sandwich sales. If she can make these additional (or *ancillary*) product sales, then she can sell far fewer than 1,020 sandwiches and still achieve her break-even point.

For example, if Sarah Sue sells regular-size beverages for $1.00, and her cost of goods sold is $.40, her gross profit on each beverage will be $.60. If she sells French fries for $1.25, and her cost of goods sold is $.35, then her gross profit on each sale is $.90. Sarah Sue may calculate the following:

Gross profit on sandwiches = $1.74

Gross profit on beverages = $ .60
 Beverages sold with 90 percent of sandwiches
 $.60 x 90% = $.54 gross profit per sandwich sale

Gross profit on French fries = $ .90
 French fries sold with 75 percent of the sandwiches
 $.90 x 75% = $.68 gross profit per sandwich sale

When she adds her gross profits together,
she gets a gross profit for a product mix:
 $1.74 + $ .54 + $ .68 = $2.96

Sarah Sue now applies her break-even formula:
 Fixed expenses ÷ gross profit = break-even point
 $1,775 ÷ $2.96 = 600

Sarah Sue can sell 600 sandwiches and achieve her break-even point, as long as she also sells beverages 90 percent of the time (600 x 90% = 540 beverages) and French fries 75 percent of the time (600 x 75% = 451 French fries). You can check your numbers by looking at them individually on this two-part worksheet:

Part 1

Gross income – COGS = **gross profit**

Sandwiches:	$3.50 – $1.76 = $1.74
Beverages:	$1.00 – $ .40 = $ .60
French fries	$1.25 – $ .35 = $ .90

Part 2

Gross profit x # sold = **total gross profit**

$1.74 x 600 = $1,044
$ .60 x 540 = $ 324
$ .90 x 451 = $ 406

Total Gross Profit:	$1,774
Total Fixed Expenses:	$1,775

This example illustrates why successful restaurants train their employees to ask, "Would you like fries with that?" each time they take an order. The difference between selling sandwiches alone (1,020 to break even) and selling sandwiches with a beverage and French fries (600 to break even) is dramatic.

If your business can't "group together" product sales, then simply make best-guess estimates of how many of each product you might sell, and keep playing with the numbers until you get a gross profit that is adequate to cover your fixed expenses.

Mary's Type

Work through the exercise below. Use the three worksheets provided. A second copy of each worksheet is provided for calculating a break-even analysis for your own business.

Mary wants to operate a secretarial service from the small business incubator near her home. Her monthly expenses would include her office rent ($150), utilities ($50), business insurance ($25), telephone service ($45), a pager ($15), and lease of office equipment ($150). Mary advertises in the local college newspaper at a cost of $20 per month. She would like to earn about $1,000 per month from her business. Mary will provide most of the labor for her business, and she calculates the cost of her own labor at $5 per hour. She assumes the following about her secretarial services:

◆ For resumes, she can charge $10 per page. An average resume is two pages long. The cost of high-quality bond paper is about $.03 per sheet. She will pay her daughter to type resumes, at a cost of $5 per hour. The average resume will take about 30 minutes to type.

◆ For term papers, Mary will charge $2 per page. An average term paper is 10 pages long. The cost of inexpensive paper is $.01 per sheet. Mary will type term papers herself. It will take her about an hour to type a 10-page term paper.

◆ Mary will charge $2 per page for business letters. The paper will be provided by each business, and she will type these herself. Each letter should take Mary about 15 minutes to type.

With the information provided above, work through Worksheets #1 through #3. On Worksheet #1, determine what Mary's fixed expenses will be. On worksheet #2, determine for each product or service what Mary's break-even points are. Finally, on worksheet # 3, finish the analysis with a reasonable product mix of services.

Tip: Include Mary's *owner's compensation* as a fixed expense. Also, include Mary's *hourly labor cost per product* as a cost of goods sold. You also should include Mary's labor here, because Mary may one day grow her business to the point where she has to hire help to produce her products. Whether the labor expense is for her or for someone else, it is important that she include it in her initial pricing calculations. As the business owner, she may not choose to pay herself an hourly rate in addition to her owner's compensation, but if she eventually hires an employee, she will have to pay that labor cost at that time.

Worksheet #1. Fixed Expenses

When identifying your monthly fixed expenses, use the average of what you expect your monthly expenses to be in the first six months. Include your target amount for owner's compensation. If you do not include your compensation in your pricing structure, you will never be able to afford to pay yourself this amount.

Fixed Expenses

Rent _____

Utilities _____

Telephone _____

Office supplies _____

Postage _____

Equipment repairs & maintenance _____

Insurance _____

Loan payments _____

Marketing costs _____

Subscriptions/Dues/Fees _____

Legal/Accounting _____

Owner's compensation _____

Other _____ _____

_____ _____

_____ _____

_____ _____

_____ _____

Total Monthly Fixed Expenses: _____

Worksheet #1. Fixed Expenses

When identifying your monthly fixed expenses, use the average of what you expect your monthly expenses to be in the first six months. Include your target amount for owner's compensation. If you do not include your compensation in your pricing structure, you will never be able to afford to pay yourself this amount.

Fixed Expenses

Rent _____

Utilities _____

Telephone _____

Office supplies _____

Postage _____

Equipment repairs & maintenance _____

Insurance _____

Loan payments _____

Marketing costs _____

Subscriptions/Dues/Fees _____

Legal/Accounting _____

Owner's compensation _____

Other _____ _____

_____ _____

_____ _____

_____ _____

_____ _____

Total Monthly Fixed Expenses: _____

Worksheet #2. Pricing/Break-Even Analysis
Individual Products

Product Name: _____

Part 1	Gross Income	–	COGC	=	Gross Profit

Part 2	Fixed Expenses	÷	Gross Profit	=	Break-Even

Product Name: _____

Part 1	Gross Income	–	COGC	=	Gross Profit

Part 2	Fixed Expenses	÷	Gross Profit	=	Break-Even

Product Name: _____

Part 1	Gross Income	–	COGC	=	Gross Profit

Part 2	Fixed Expenses	÷	Gross Profit	=	Break-Even

Worksheet #2. Pricing/Break-Even Analysis
Individual Products

Product Name: _____

Part 1   Gross Income   –   COGC   =   Gross Profit

Part 2   Fixed Expenses   ÷   Gross Profit   =   Break-Even

Product Name: _____

Part 1   Gross Income   –   COGC   =   Gross Profit

Part 2   Fixed Expenses   ÷   Gross Profit   =   Break-Even

Product Name: _____

Part 1   Gross Income   –   COGC   =   Gross Profit

Part 2   Fixed Expenses   ÷   Gross Profit   =   Break-Even

Worksheet #3. Pricing/Break-Even Analysis
Product Mix

Part 1: Income – COGS = Gross Profit

	Income	COGS	Gross Profit
Product #1			
Product #2			
Product #3			
Product #4			
Total Products			

Total Fixed Expenses $_____

Part 2: Gross Profit x # sold = Total Gross Profit

	Gross Profit	# sold	Total Gross Profit
Product #1			
Product #2			
Product #3			
Product #4			
Total Products			

Total Fixed Expenses $_____

Worksheet #3. Pricing/Break-Even Analysis
Product Mix

Part 1: Income – COGS = Gross Profit

	Income	COGS	Gross Profit
Product #1			
Product #2			
Product #3			
Product #4			
Total Products			

Total Fixed Expenses $_____

Part 2:	Gross Profit	x	# sold	=	Total Gross Profit
Product #1					
Product #2					
Product #3					
Product #4					
Total Products					
Total Fixed Expenses					$_____

Pricing for Service Providers

This formula (and the following worksheet) can be used to determine an appropriate hourly billing rate for a service provider. Service providers may include consultants, designers, technicians, writers, and other small businesses that primarily sell their time.

Step 1. Determine your income requirements. Estimate your annual operating expenses (sometimes called *overhead*). These should include things like rent, utilities, insurance, and telephone service.

Next, decide how much personal income you need to earn. Don't forget to include the cost of self-employment tax, your estimated federal tax liability, and the cost of health insurance premiums.

Annual operating expenses:	$10,000
Owner's gross wages:	$30,000
Total income requirements:	$40,000

Step 2. Calculate available working hours. Multiply the number of weeks per year by the number of work hours per week.

52 weeks x 40 hours per week: 2,080 total hours

Subtract time off for annual vacations and holidays to get your total available work hours per year.

—40 vacation hours and 56 holiday hours: 2,080 − 96 = 1,984 available hours

Step 3. Estimate billable hours. Estimate what percentage of your available time you will be able to bill clients. Consider your expectations for gaining new jobs or new clients over time. This percentage may have seasonal fluctuations, depending on your business. Break down these estimates by months or quarters.

1,984 hours available per year
1,984 ÷ 4 = 496 hours available per quarter

	Available Hours	x	Percentage Billable Hours	=	Billable Hours per Quarter
Quarter 1:	496	x	20% (1 day per week)		99
Quarter 2:	496	x	25% (1 out of 4 days)		124
Quarter 3:	496	x	30% (1 out of 3 days)		149
Quarter 4:	496	x	40% (2 days per week)		198
Estimated Billable Hours:					570

Step 4. **Calculate your hourly billing rate.** Divide your total required income (from Step 1) by the number of estimated billable hours per year (from Step 3) to get your hourly rate.

$40,000 ÷ 570 hours = $70.18 per hour

Step 5. **Decide if the rate seems reasonable.** Does the rate seem reasonable? Consider what the market will bear. Your answer depends on the type of service you provide and your competition. If the rate is not reasonable, how can you adjust it? Is your salary goal too high? Can you reduce overhead expenses or increase billable hours? Can you accomplish this amount of work and manage your business while maintaining a reasonable schedule? Is this a viable business given your financial and lifestyle goals?

Service Providers/Hourly Rate Worksheet

Annual Operating Expenses

Rent	_____
Utilities	+ _____
Telephone	+ _____
Office supplies	+ _____
Postage	+ _____
Equipment repairs & maintenance	+ _____
Business insurance	+ _____
Loan payments	+ _____
Marketing costs	+ _____
Subscriptions/Dues/Fees	+ _____
Legal/Accounting	+ _____

Travel & entertainment   + _____

Other _____   + _____

_____   _____

_____   _____

_____   _____

_____   _____

Total annual operating expenses: = _____

Owner's annual compensation: + _____

Self-employment taxes: + _____

Annual health insurance cost: + _____

#1. Total income required: = _____

Total working hours per year   2,080
(52 weeks x 40 hours)

Less vacation hours: −_____

Less holiday hours: −_____

#2. Available working hours per year   = _____

Available working hours per quarter   = _____
(available hours per year ÷ 4)

Estimated Billable Hours per Quarter

	Available Hours per Quarter		Percent Billable Hours		# Billable Hours per Quarter
Quarter 1:	_____	x	_____	=	_____
Quarter 2:	_____	x	_____	=	_____
Quarter 3:	_____	x	_____	=	_____
Quarter 4:	_____	x	_____	=	_____

#3. Estimated billable hours per year: = _____

#4. Total income ÷ **total billable** = **hourly rate:** = _____
required   **hours per year**

#5. Is this reasonable?

Summing Up

After you have completed your analysis, ask yourself the following questions:

◆ **Does your pricing seems reasonable?** Consider what the market will bear. The answer depends on the products you are providing and your competition.

◆ **If your prices are not reasonable, can you adjust them?** Can you minimize your cost of goods sold without sacrificing quality? Can you reduce your fixed expenses? If so, how? Is your owner's compensation goal too high? Are there fixed expenses that can be eliminated? If your expenses cannot be reduced substantially, can your estimated sales be reasonably increased?

◆ **Taking into account your local competition, are your sales goals reasonable?** Also take into account your business hours. Are your sales estimates reasonable for the number of hours your business will be open?

◆ **If you will be providing the bulk of the labor, how many hours will it take for you to meet your production goals?** In the example of Mary's secretarial service, she may determine that she will have to work more hours for less personal income to become self-employed. If this is the case for you, ask yourself if that is consistent with your financial and lifestyle goals. Can you accomplish this amount of work *and* manage your business while maintaining a reasonable schedule?

The answers to these questions will help you decide if your business idea is a viable one.

Once you've made the commitment to start your business, track your actual expenses and sales. Compare your actual numbers to your original estimates. Review these numbers often, and adjust your estimates accordingly. The longer your business operates, the more information you will have and the better your estimates will become.

Finding Your Market

*M*any people dream of starting a business so they can make a living doing work they do well and that they love doing. But when you are just starting out, you'll find that you spend most of your time trying to find people who will pay you for your work. Although you are good at your chosen occupation, you may be uncomfortable when it comes to marketing your business. But marketing is one of the most important things you will do, not only as you start but as you continue to run your businesses.

What does it mean to market your business? When you hear the word *marketing*, you may think of advertising, promotions, public relations, or market research. And, indeed, marketing includes all of these. It sounds complicated and expensive. Some marketing departments in large corporations do have enormous budgets. But you can make your marketing efforts fun and inexpensive. Remember, you only get a chance to *sell* your product or service to your customers when they *know* about your product or service.

Step-by-Step Marketing

Step 1. Know Your Product

The first step in developing a marketing plan is to be very clear about what you are selling. You must be able to describe your product or service in clear, precise terms that anyone can understand. Before you can sell your product or service to a potential customer, *you* must be convinced that what you offer is terrific. Below are some questions that will start you thinking about the best way to describe your product or service.

◆ What product or service do you provide? Don't forget to include support services you offer (for example, delivery, maintenance, and house calls).

_____

_____

◆ What makes your product or service special? How is your product or service different from ones that are already on the market?

_____

_____

> **Marketing means making potential customers aware of your product or service.**

◆ Why will people want to buy your product or service?

_____

_____

◆ Add any other information about your product or service you think is important.

_____

_____

One of the biggest mistakes beginning entrepreneurs make is not having a clear product or service to sell. They try to sell something to everyone. Their message becomes lost and they confuse the consumer. As your business grows, you may be able to expand your services and products. But in the beginning, it's crucial to:

◆ Focus!

◆ Focus!

◆ Focus!

Below are examples of entrepreneurs and their products and services. Read through the examples and check those who are ready to begin marketing to their potential customers.

_____ A florist who does not provide a delivery service.

_____ A small clothing store that offers punk styles, business outfits, maternity clothes, and formals.

_____ A seamstress who sews new clothes and does alterations for middle-income women. She will make house calls or do fittings at her workshop by appointment.

_____ A hairdresser who works alone, trying to develop a walk-in business and do home visits at the same time.

_____ A caterer with excellent home-cooked food who puts care into arranging beautiful table displays. She does not provide servers, but has a list of people she can recommend.

_____ An upholsterer who does the sewing and refinishing but expects customers to bring their own material.

_____ An experienced daycare provider who offers educational toys, snacks, a play area, and flexible hours.

_____ A delivery service that promises next-day delivery but does not pick up after noon.

_____ A single person doing roofing, indoor/outdoor painting, carpentry, and household repairs.

_____ A landscaper offering landscape design, a 15 percent discount arrangement with the local garden center, delivery, installation, and maintenance.

_____ A house painter emphasizing quality work but using a cheap grade of paint to save customers money.

Step 2. Know Your Customers

The second step in developing a marketing plan is to determine who your potential customers are. You have limited time and money, so it's important to target your resources to the people who are most likely to buy from you.

When you think of your product or service, what common characteristics do you think your potential customers might have? If your customers will be organizations, what characteristics will they have in common?

_____

_____

_____

_____

Here are some characteristics to help you get started.

Individuals

Income level	Job and position
Sex, age, marital status	Religion
Education	Location
Health	Hobbies, skills
Do-it-yourself types	Internal capabilities
Race	Number of children
Own or rent a home	Age and type of car
Vacation activities	Household pets
Eating habits, buying habits	

Organizations

Size
Profit/Not-for-profit
Number of employees
Location

Now that you've identified who your potential customers will be, let's look at what may be important to them.

What Are Your Customers Looking For?

Below is a list of qualities customers look for in products and services. Scan through them; then list in the space provided the three things you think are *the* most important to customers who would buy your product or service.

1. _____

2 _____

3. _____

☞ Durability   ☞ Style   ☞ Cost

☞ Variety   ☞ Promptness   ☞ Reliability

☞ Ease of care   ☞ Efficiency   ☞ Comfort

☞ Craftsmanship

Check Out the Market

There are several sources of information on the business community and customer base in your area. Check out these first; then brainstorm to come up with other possibilities.

◆ **The public library:** You can get information on the size and make-up of your market, the number of people per household, family income, the number of homeowners and home values, and the number of cars per household. This kind of information is available for both the national and local levels, so you can compare the two. Here are some of the information sources you will find at your local library:

    🙾 *Encyclopedia of Associations* lists trade associations, including addresses and phone numbers and a list of publications.

    🙾 *Measuring Markets: A Guide to the Use of Federal and State Statistical Data* will help you find specific publications with market information for the area that interests you.

    🙾 *Census of Population and Housing, Standard Metropolitan Statistical Areas,* and *Census Tract Reports.*

- 🕭 *County Business Patterns* summarizes information on businesses by state, and county. Information is provided by business type, number and size of businesses, and number of employees.

◆ The *Yellow Pages*

◆ **Competitors:** Check out your competition's marketing literature and publicity; observe their customers and how customers are treated; look at the same type of business in another community or town.

◆ **Wholesalers and manufacturers**

◆ **Federal and state governments**

◆ **Business, trade, and professional journals and meetings**

◆ **Chambers of commerce and local governments**

◆ **Potential customers:** Watch your potential customers in action, or do interview surveys with them.

Step 3. Get the Word Out

So now you've defined your product or service and you have an idea of who your customers will be. In this section, we'll look at several ways to make those potential customers aware of your product or service. Certain ideas will work better for some businesses than for others. However, there is one idea every entrepreneur should remember: Business is about relationships!

In most cases, it takes time for potential customers to become paying customers. In your personal life you do not meet a person, spend a few minutes with him or her, and immediately become best friends. It's the same in business; it takes time for potential customers to understand and believe in the benefits of your product or service. As you spread the word about your product or service, you will meet lots of people who are interested in your business but who don't need or want to buy from you at that time. Consider and work with these people as potential customers.

Let's begin with some simple ways to make your potential customers aware of your product or service and to encourage them to buy from you. Keep your profile of potential customers in mind as you consider these ideas.

Create a Professional Image

Earlier, we discussed the importance of a good name for your business. But there is more to creating an image than a name. Should you also consider a logo? What written materials will you need? Business cards? Stationary? Brochures? Your business image comes across strongly on the phone. Think about how you will answer the phone and consider the image you want to give. If you have employees who answer the phones, you must take time to explain to them the image you are trying to create. You need to be sure everything about your business reflects that *you are a professional*.

Many businesses today are located in private homes, and customers either don't know or don't care. However, if your business is located in your home and you are worried that it might make potential customers unsure if you can handle their business, you might consider renting a post office box or adding a suite number to your home address. You might also pay a little extra for a phone number that sounds businesslike (595-1000).

> *Make sure you offer only what your market wants to buy.*

To get started thinking about your professional image, write your answer to this question in the space below: "What does your image need to say to your potential customers?"

_____

_____

_____

_____

_____

_____

Network

Networking is a hot topic these days. We are acutely aware of the importance of networking to find a job, or even perhaps a mate, but you should use networking to market your business, too. That means being prepared to talk about your business to anyone and everyone. Your car mechanic may not be interested in buying your product or service, but his brother-in-law might become your best customer. Remember, business is about relationships. Always carry your business cards with you, and when you hand them out, give people two: one for themselves and one for someone they know who might be interested in your product or service. Below are some more ideas to get you started networking.

◆ Become the expert in your field.

◆ Always do what you say you will do.

◆ Create a follow-up system so you will remember who and when to call.

◆ Stay in touch with previous customers.

◆ Always send thank-you notes.

◆ Follow up with a phone call after a week to be sure your customers are pleased with your product or service.

◆ Seize each and every opportunity.

◆ Consider "freebies" if they could mean sales in the future.

◆ Make networking calls every week.

◆ Join professional groups.

◆ Volunteer in local organizations.

Advertise

Most small businesses don't have the money to pay for an advertising blitz. The good news is that most small businesses don't need to advertise on a large scale. You probably will be better off if you appeal *directly to your target customers* by less expensive means. If your business must advertise to larger markets, you should proceed carefully. Many microenterprises have lost vast amounts of money with no return by choosing the wrong advertising vehicles. You might attract more customers with a well-thought-out brochure mailed to people you *know* are potential customers than with an ad run once in a newspaper.

There are some basics you should keep in mind, however you choose to advertise:

◆ Make your message consistent.

◆ Create a learning experience for your customers.

◆ The secret to marketing is repetition.

◆ Try to create an element of surprise and fun.

Below are some advertising methods you might consider. Some are more feasible than others for small businesses, but don't discount any of them without exploring all the possibilities.

◆ **Television** ads are short and fleeting, and it's difficult to be sure you're going to hit your target market. They also may be too expensive for your small business, but check with local cable stations before you completely rule them out. Cable stations are less expensive and may appeal to an audience that is close to your potential market. Local talk shows also may be perfect for your topic; many interview "experts" on a variety of topics. *You* may be the expert in your field.

◆ **Radio** also is expensive, but it's easier to get directly to your target market. Remember, however, that radio usually is background noise, so an ad on the radio takes many repetitions before people actually hear your message. Again, talk shows can be helpful in getting your message out.

◆ **Print advertising** includes ads in either magazines or newspapers. If you do some careful research, *you can get directly to your customers* with this medium. The impact of print, however, may build more slowly than other kinds of advertising. If your customers will contact you by phone to request your product or service, you might consider an ad in the *Yellow Pages*. Look at your competitors' ads. But keep this question in mind: How many customers each month will you need from that ad to make it cost-effective?

◆ **The press release** is a time-honored way of telling people you're in business. And you don't have to hire a professional to write one. Check your library for information on how a press release should look and what information it should include. Often local media are looking for good stories, so try to present your company as newsworthy. And don't forget to follow up with a phone call to answer questions about your press release. If appropriate, have your services listed in the calendar of events in your local newspaper or in any listing about changes in companies.

◆ **Mail** is one of the cheapest ways to get your information into the hands of your customers, but it also is one of the more difficult methods of advertising. If you are going to create a large direct-mail campaign and you don't want your hard work to get thrown out with the junk mail, you need to either thoroughly research your project or hire professional help. If you are mailing to your past customers and your own list of potential customers, always remember to maintain a professional image. Again, consult books in the library on setting up a direct-mail campaign.

◆ **Trade shows** are worth considering if you can find one geared to your product or services. Common estimates say that 86 percent of trade show attendees are there to buy. Your goal should be to meet as many people as possible, so you can develop sales leads. Have a system to take names and addresses to add to your customer database, and be sure to follow up on all leads soon after the show.

◆ **Word of mouth** is probably the best advertising you can have, because your satisfied customers effectively become your sales force. It doesn't cost anything, but this method of marketing takes a while to develop.

Check Out the Competition

In his book *The Start Up Guide*, David Bangs, Jr., tells a story about the early days of television.[1] Hollywood executives decided they were in the business of making movies, and that television wasn't any competition. After several years of losing millions of dollars and several closed studios, Hollywood moguls finally learned they were in *the entertainment business,* and that they did, indeed, have to compete with "the little box."

Who are your competitors? Is your competition trying to appeal to the same customers you are? Your answer to your competitors is simple: Create a niche. Your niche can be who you serve, what you do, where you do it, when you do it, or how you do it, or it can combine any of those factors. In the following space, list your competitors and identify their strengths and weaknesses. How do you compare with the competition on price, location, quality, service, and image?

My Competitors

Strengths   **Weaknesses**

_____   _____

_____   _____

_____   _____

_____   _____

Similar products or services are competition unless they appeal to the same market. A small dress-making business catering to middle-class customers probably is not in competition with the local thrift shop or the designer floor of the downtown department store. But it might face serious competition from middle-range mail-order fashion catalogs.

If customers do not buy your product, where else can they find what they're looking for? Although another business may not be selling exactly the same product or service as yours, you may still consider it competition if it is providing an alternative way for the customers to meet their needs.

For example, instead of hiring your phone-answering service, customers might buy answering machines; arrange with friends, family members, or colleagues to take messages; use call-forwarding; or make do without having calls answered. Choosing any one of these options prevents the customer from choosing your answering service. In the space below, jot down any competitors you need to consider.

Indirect competition I should consider:

_____

_____

_____

_____

The Customer *Is* Always Right

Finally, whenever you think about dealing with your customers, potential or actual, remember that good customer service can mean the difference between business success and failure. If you have trouble believing that, consider these facts:

◆ **Customers *will* tell a company where it needs improvement.** Ask your customers how you can make your business more suitable to them, *and then listen to what they say!*

◆ **Poor service is the #1 reason American companies lose business.** Most customers stop doing business with a company because of poor service.

◆ **The majority of customers who stop doing business with a company make no attempt to tell the firm why.**

◆ **Only a minority of dissatisfied customers never complain.** Most dissatisfied customers don't complain because they believe: (1) it's not worth their time, (2) the company won't listen, or (3) the company won't do anything about the complaint.

◆ **The average dissatisfied customer tells many people about his or her dissatisfaction.**

◆ **According to quality guru Tom Peters, it takes $10 of new business to replace $1 of lost business.**[2]

◆ **Quality of service is the main thing that differentiates one business from another.**

◆ **Customers are willing to pay more for better service.**

Summing Up

You may have the best product or service in your area, but if you have no customers, you will not be able to make money and maintain your business. The time to educate yourself about your product and your potential customers is *before* you begin your business. Ask lots of questions and *listen* to what people tell you. Remember, you are beginning to make business relationships, so it is always important to do what you tell people you will do.

Notes

1. David Bangs, Jr., *The Start Up Guide: A One Year Plan for Entrepreneurs* (Dover, NH: Upstart Publishing Company, 1994).

2. Tom Peters and R. Waterman, *In Search of Excellence* (New York: Warner Books, 1982).

Managing Your Cash Flow

Successful business owners know how to manage the flow of cash coming into and going out of their businesses. They realize that even a profitable business can fail if there is no operating cash available. Skillful cash-flow management results from proper planning. By making some simple forecasts, you can learn to project your cash-flow requirements. Experience will improve your ability to create sound cash-flow projections.

In this chapter, you will learn to create useful projections to help you manage your cash flow.

What Is Cash Flow?

Cash flow, as the name implies, is simply the flow of cash coming into and going out of your business. You achieve positive cash flow when money comes into your business faster than it goes out. Since a business must have cash to operate, you must maintain positive cash flow in order to survive. Positive cash flow is a matter of timing. Managing your cash flow is a matter of planning.

Having cash is not the same as being profitable. It is possible for a business to have cash and be operating at a loss. For example, if you start your business with $10,000 in the bank, and you operate at a loss of $1,000 each month, how many months can you stay in business and have cash in the bank? It also is possible for a business to be making a profit and have no cash. For example, if you are operating at a profit, extending 60-day credit terms to your customers, but paying your suppliers upon delivery, how long will you be able to keep operating before you run out of cash?

This is important to understand, because many small business owners believe that as long as they have cash in the bank, they must be making a profit. That can be a dangerous assumption.

Small business owners tend to neglect the task of business management. There are many important things a business owner must do: make sales, produce products, provide services, compete for customers. Owners often spend so much time "being" the business, they don't take time to "manage" the business. This is a common mistake that results in the business "managing" the owner.

> **Manage your business, or your business will manage you.**

For a business owner, cash-flow management is one task you probably will face daily. If you don't start with a plan, you'll spend a great deal of time reacting to instead of anticipating events. You may find yourself trying to placate suppliers, struggling to make loan payments, hoping for a miracle so you can make payroll, and losing sleep over how to keep your utilities from being disconnected (again). The result is that you have even less time to make sales, produce products, provide services, and compete for customers—plus you will have strained important relationships with your creditors. In the long run, you create more stress for yourself if you don't manage your business. Avoid the trap of being managed by your business: Learn to manage your cash flow.

Projecting Cash Flow

Cathy's Cleaning Service

Cathy Smith owns a residential and commercial cleaning business. She has four employees (one of whom is her mother) who work in two cleaning crews. Each crew works the same monthly schedule, cleaning two commercial buildings and seven homes.

Cathy also cleans newly constructed homes for a local builder and vacated apartments for a property management company. She cleans these herself.

Her residential customers pay for cleaning services as they are performed by leaving checks for the crews to deliver to Cathy at the end of each day. The two commercial buildings are invoiced once a month with 30-day terms. Cathy invoices the construction company and property manager as she cleans for them, and they usually pay her within 15 days.

Cathy reimburses her employees for mileage expenses to travel to job sites. She includes these reimbursements with the paychecks each Friday afternoon.

Cathy has no cash-flow plan; she is much too busy cleaning to create one each month.

Let's look at Cathy's cash flow for the month of August.

Cathy's Cleaning Service, Before ...

	Ending Bank Balance
### Week 1	
Cathy starts the week with $75.	$ 75.00
1. She collects $180 from residential homes.	$255.00
2. Cathy gets a check for $280 for new homes cleaned two weeks ago.	$535.00
3. Payroll this week is $435.	$100.00
4. Mileage reimbursements total $25.	$ 75.00
5. Cathy needs $12.50 to fill her gas tank.	$ 62.50
Cathy ends week one with $62.50.	$ 62.50

Week 2

6. Residential homes pay $225 this week.	$287.50
7. A new home Cathy cleaned two weeks ago pays $70.	$357.50
8. Payroll is $435, which leaves Cathy short. She asks her mother not to cash her check, but her mother cannot afford to do this.	$ (77.50)
9. Mileage reimbursements are $27. Cathy isn't sure what to do.	$(104.50)
Cathy ends the week with a negative bank balance, and worries that the checks will hit the bank before she can cover them.	$(104.50)

Week 3

10. Cathy hears from the bank immediately: Her account is charged an $18 NSF.	$(122.50)
11. Cathy borrows $150 from a friend, who is not happy about it.	$ 27.50
12. Residential homes pay $180.	$207.50
13. Building No. 2 pays $350 for one month.	$557.50
14. Payroll this week is $435. Employees murmur and rush to the bank.	$122.50
15. Mileage reimbursements are an additional $26.	$ 96.50
16. Cathy must spend $50 on cleaning supplies.	$ 46.50
17. Cathy needs $12.50 for gas for her car.	$ 34.00
18. An apartment she cleaned last month pays her $75.	$109.00
Cathy ends this week with $109, an angry friend, upset employees, and a serious headache.	$109.00

Week 4

19. Cathy collects $225 from residential customers.	$334.00
20. Building No. 1 pays a $500 monthly cleaning bill.	$834.00
21. Payroll is $435, and Cathy is thrilled she has the cash.	$399.00
22. Cathy's angry friend insists on repayment of the $150 loan *now*!	$249.00
23. Mileage reimbursements total $26.	$223.00
24. A new home Cathy cleaned two weeks ago pays $100.	$323.00
25. Cathy needs gas for her car again: $12.50.	$310.50
26. Cathy finally pays herself a salary for the month: $200.	$110.50
Cathy ends the month with $110.50 and the dread of facing another month of similar struggles!	$110.50

Cathy Makes a Plan

1. Cathy knows how much and when she will collect from residential customers.

2. Cathy's payroll amount remains about the same each week.

3. Her commercial accounts are on contract and pay the same amount each month.

4. Cathy knows how much she will have to reimburse her employees for mileage.

5. Cathy can make an educated guess about how much income she will collect from cleaning new houses and vacant apartments. She also can ask the new homes builder and the apartment manager to give her an estimate at the beginning of each month, since they know when they will need her weeks before they call her.

Given all that Cathy knows and can assume, she can draw a "picture" of when cash is going to come in and when it is going out. It would look like the table below.

Cathy's Cleaning Service

Date	Description	Cash In	Cash Out	Balance
				$75.00
Week 1	Homes	$180.00		$255.00
	New Homes	$280.00		$535.00
	Payroll		$435.00	$100.00
	Mileage		$25.00	$75.00
	Gasoline		$12.50	$62.50
Week 2	Homes	$225.00		$287.50
	New Home	$70.00		$357.50
	Payroll		$435.00	($77.50)
	Mileage		$27.00	($104.50)
Week 3	NSF		$18.00	($122.50)
	Loan	$150.00		$27.50
	Homes	$180.00		$207.50
	Building #2	$350.00		$557.50
	Payroll		$435.00	$122.50
	Mileage		$26.00	$96.50
	Cleaning Sup		$50.00	$46.50
	Gasoline		$12.50	$34.00
	Apartment	$75.00		$109.00
Week 4	Homes	$225.00		$334.00
	Building #1	$500.00		$834.00
	Payroll		$435.00	$399.00
	Repay Loan		$150.00	$249.00
	Mileage		$26.00	$223.00
	New Home	$100.00		$323.00
	Gasoline		$12.50	$310.50
	Cathy		$200.00	$110.50
		$2,335.00	$2,299.50	$110.50

Without any plan, Cathy didn't know she was going to run out of cash. Once she created her plan, she was able to come up with some short-term solutions for her anticipated cash shortages. More importantly, Cathy has seen the need to come up with some long-term solutions to avoid future shortages.

Here are some other ideas that might help Cathy improve her cash-flow plan.

1. Cathy invoices her commercial customers only once a month, even though she cleans for them every week. They pay her invoices according to her terms: within 30 days. Cathy could start sending invoices on a weekly basis. The invoice amounts would be smaller (one week of cleaning instead of one month), but the payments would come in faster.

Positive cash flow is a matter of timing.

2. Cathy pays her employees and reimburses their mileage expenses once a week. She could change her payroll and mileage reimbursements to once every two weeks (26 times per year) or, better yet, twice a month (24 times per year). This would allow Cathy to hold onto her cash longer.

3. Instead of paying for her supplies in cash, Cathy could establish credit accounts with her primary suppliers. Again, Cathy would hold on to her cash longer.

In the tables that follow, you can see the effects of these three simple changes on Cathy's cash flow.

Notice that Cathy didn't collect any *more* cash from her commercial accounts, she just collected it *faster*. She did not pay her employees any less, she just held onto her cash longer. Cathy still was able to buy cleaning supplies when she needed them, she just deferred payment.

As a result of these changes, Cathy didn't bounce any payroll checks, which made her employees happy. She didn't need to borrow money from her friend, which made her friend happy. She avoided the bank's NSF charges, which made her bank happy. And she was left with considerably higher cash balances at the end of each week, which made Cathy very happy. She also begins the new month with a higher cash balance and a management plan.

Predicting the (Cash) Future

It doesn't take a crystal ball to project your cash future. What it does take is some educated guessing. The longer you are in business and the more experience you acquire, the better your guesses will be.

Cathy's Cleaning Service, Before...

Date	Description	Deposits	Checks	Balance
Week 1				$75.00
	Homes	$180.00		$255.00
	New Homes	$280.00		$535.00
	Payroll		$435.00	$100.00
	Mileage		$25.00	$75.00
	Gasoline		$12.50	$62.50
Week 2				
	Homes	$225.00		$287.50
	New Home	$70.00		$357.50
	Payroll		$435.00	($77.50)
	Mileage		$27.00	($104.50)
Week 3				
	NSF		$18.00	($122.50)
	Loan	$150.00		$27.50
	Homes	$180.00		$207.50
	Building 2	$350.00		$557.50
	Payroll		$435.00	$122.50
	Mileage		$26.00	$96.50
	Cleaning Sup		$50.00	$46.50
	Gasoline		$12.50	$34.00
	Apartment	$75.00		$109.00
Week 4				
	Homes	$225.00		$334.00
	Building #1	$500.00		$834.00
	Payroll		$435.00	$399.00
	Repay Loan		$150.00	$249.00
	Mileage		$26.00	$223.00
	New Home	$100.00		$323.00
	Gasoline		$12.50	$310.50
	Cathy		$200.00	$110.50
		$2,335.00	$2,299.50	$110.50

Cathy's Cleaning Service, After...

Date	Description	Deposits	Checks	Balance
Week 1				$75.00
	Homes	$180.00		$255.00
	New Homes	$280.00		$535.00
	Building #1	$125.00		$660.00
	Building #2	$87.50		$747.50
	Gasoline		$12.50	$735.00
Week 2				
	Homes	$225.00		$960.00
	New Home	$70.00		$1,030.00
	Building #1	$125.00		$1,155.00
	Building #2	$87.50		$1,242.50
	Payroll/2 wks		$870.00	$372.50
	Mileage/2 wks		$52.00	$320.50
Week 3				
	Homes	$180.00		$500.50
	Building #1	$125.00		$625.50
	Building #2	$87.50		$713.00
	Apartment	$75.00		$788.00
	Gasoline		$12.50	$775.50
Week 4				
	Homes	$225.00		$1,000.50
	Building #1	$125.00		$1,125.50
	Building #2	$87.50		$1,213.00
	Payroll/2 wks		$870.00	$343.00
	Mileage/2 wks		$52.00	$291.00
	New Home	$100.00		$391.00
	Gasoline		$12.50	$378.50
	Cathy		$200.00	$178.50
		$2,185.00	$2,081.50	$178.50

To create cash-flow projections, take the information you know plus information you assume and apply it to a calendar or a time line. Not all businesses are as predictable as Cathy's Cleaning Service. Some information may be easy to predict: For example, your rent is a fixed amount that is due on the first day of each month; your telephone bill is usually $150, due on the 25th; and your insurance premiums are payable once a quarter. Other information is more difficult to forecast: How much will sale revenues be in January? Will this be a harsh winter with extraordinarily high heating bills? Will you suffer costly equipment failures?

When preparing your cash-flow projections, there are other things to consider, as well. Will seasonal fluctuations, holidays, or events in your community have an impact on your business? Will a convention in town mean more or less business for you? What about sporting events? How about plans for road construction? Will the weather affect your business? What about annual conventions for your industry?

Whether you are establishing a new business or managing an existing one, think of ways to stretch your dollars to improve your cash flow. This might mean renegotiating credit terms with customers or suppliers. If this is the case, schedule time to do it. Remember, time spent managing your business ensures that your business does not manage you!

Be creative! List ways you can create a positive cash flow for your business:

_____

_____

_____

_____

_____

_____

_____

_____

_____

_____

_____

_____

Sandra's Sewing Circle

In this exercise, account for start-up cash flow in and start-up cash flow out; then estimate four consecutive weeks of operation in a new business. Complete the worksheet using these assumptions:

1. Sandra's Sewing Circle begins with a cash balance of $0.00. She will make an owner's investment of $1,000, and add a no-interest loan from her mother of $500.

2. Sandra will have to pay an $80 deposit to the phone company for service, as well as a $50 business license fee to the city.

3. Sandra will purchase $450 of start-up inventory. She already owns most of her own equipment, and she is setting up her business in a friend's shop.

4. Sandra is now ready to start estimating her operating expenses. In the first week, Sandra will begin paying her friend $40 a week for rent. Sandra thinks she will do $120 of business, for which she will be paid in cash. Sandra will have to pay $75 for a previous delivery of business cards and stationery. She estimates an additional purchase of fabrics for $40.

5. In her second week of business, Sandra estimates income of $145. She estimates her share of the electric bill will be $20. She knows she will have an insurance premium of $75. Sandra wants to draw $150 for her own salary. Additional fabrics should be around $50.

6. In week 3, Sandra hopes to bring in $200 of sales income from a high school band account, as well as $45 of retail business. She will pay for her ad in the neighborhood newspaper, which will cost $25. She estimates a purchase of fabrics at a cost of $75.

7. Sandra estimates income of only $120 in week 4. Sandra will have to pay her mother $200 against her loan this week. She also wants to pay herself another $150. Sandra estimates her telephone bill at $60 and additional fabrics at $40.

On the following pages are two start-up cash-flow worksheets and two cash-flow worksheets for an existing business. Complete the first start-up worksheet using the information about Sandra's Sewing Circle. Use the other worksheets to make cash-flow projections for your own business.

Start-Up Business Cash-Flow Worksheet

		Start-up cash flow	Week 1	Week 2	Week 3	Week 4
1.	**Beginning cash**					
	Cash in:					
2.	Owner's investment					
3.	Loan proceeds					
4.	Sales income					
5.	Other: _____					
6.	**Total cash in (add lines 2–5)**					
	Cash out/start-up					
7.	Initial rent/deposits					
8.	Initial utility/deposits					
9.	Equipment purchases/deposits					
10.	Initial inventory purchases					
11.	Initial office supply purchases					
12.	Fees/License					
13.	Other: _____					
14.	Other: _____					
	Cash out/monthly					
15.	COGS, labor					
16.	COGS, materials					
17.	Rent					
18.	Insurance					
19.	Payroll					
20.	Payroll taxes					
21.	Loan payments					
22.	Advertising/Marketing					
23.	Travel expenses					
24.	Owner's compensation					
25.	Office supplies					
26.	Telephone					
27.	Utilities					
28.	Other: _____					
29.	Other: _____					
30.	Other: _____					
31.	Other: _____					
32.	Other: _____					
33.	**Total cash out (add lines 7–32)**					
34.	**Change in cash (line 6 minus line 33)**					
35.	**Ending cash (line 1 plus line 34)**					

Note: *Ending cash for one period becomes the beginning cash for the next period.*

Start-Up Business Cash-Flow Worksheet

		Start-up cash flow	Week 1	Week 2	Week 3	Week 4
1.	**Beginning cash**					
	Cash in:					
2.	Owner's investment					
3.	Loan proceeds					
4.	Sales income					
5.	Other: _____					
6.	**Total cash in (add lines 2–5)**					
	Cash out/start-up					
7.	Initial rent/deposits					
8.	Initial utility/deposits					
9.	Equipment purchases/deposits					
10.	Initial inventory purchases					
11.	Initial office supply purchases					
12.	Fees/License					
13.	Other: _____					
14.	Other: _____					
	Cash out/monthly					
15.	COGS, labor					
16.	COGS, materials					
17.	Rent					
18.	Insurance					
19.	Payroll					
20.	Payroll taxes					
21.	Loan payments					
22.	Advertising/Marketing					
23.	Travel expenses					
24.	Owner's compensation					
25.	Office supplies					
26.	Telephone					
27.	Utilities					
28.	Other: _____					
29.	Other: _____					
30.	Other: _____					
31.	Other: _____					
32.	Other: _____					
33.	**Total cash out (add lines 7–32)**					
34.	**Change in cash (line 6 minus line 33)**					
35.	**Ending cash (line 1 plus line 34)**					

Note: Ending cash for one period becomes the beginning cash for the next period.

Existing Business Cash-Flow Worksheet

		Period 1		Period 2		Period 3	
		Projected	Actual	Projected	Actual	Projected	Actual
1.	**Beginning cash**						
	Cash in:						
2.	Owner's investment						
3.	Loan proceeds						
4.	Sales income						
5.	Other: _____						
6.	**Total cash in** (add lines 2–5)						
	Cash out/monthly						
7.	COGS, labor						
8.	COGS, materials						
9.	Rent						
10.	Insurance						
11.	Payroll						
12.	Payroll taxes						
13.	Loan payments						
14.	Advertising/Marketing						
15.	Travel expenses						
16.	Owner's compensation						
17.	Office supplies						
18.	Telephone						
19.	Utilities						
20.	Other: _____						
21.	Other: _____						
22.	Other: _____						
23.	Other: _____						
24.	Other: _____						
25.	**Total cash out** (add lines 7–24)						
26.	**Change in cash** (line 6 minus line 25)						
27.	**Ending cash** (line 1 plus line 26)						

Note: Ending cash for one period becomes the beginning cash for the next period.

Existing Business Cash-Flow Worksheet

		Period 1		Period 2		Period 3	
		Projected	Actual	Projected	Actual	Projected	Actual
1.	Beginning cash						
	Cash in:						
2.	Owner's investment						
3.	Loan proceeds						
4.	Sales income						
5.	Other: _____						
6.	Total cash in (add lines 2–5)						
	Cash out/monthly						
7.	COGS, labor						
8.	COGS, materials						
9.	Rent						
10.	Insurance						
11.	Payroll						
12.	Payroll taxes						
13.	Loan payments						
14.	Advertising/Marketing						
15.	Travel expenses						
16.	Owner's compensation						
17.	Office supplies						
18.	Telephone						
19.	Utilities						
20.	Other: _____						
21.	Other: _____						
22.	Other: _____						
23.	Other: _____						
24.	Other: _____						
25.	Total cash out (add lines 7–24)						
26.	Change in cash (line 6 minus line 25)						
27.	Ending cash (line 1 plus line 26)						

Note: *Ending cash for one period becomes the beginning cash for the next period.*

What Does Your Lender Want?

If you intend to approach a lender for funds, a cash-flow projection, or financial plan (see Chapter 3), will be one of the most important documents you submit. You should make your cash-flow projection for at least one year, maybe longer, depending on the requirements of the lender.

It is common for a start-up business to show negative cash balances in the first year. Most lenders expect your projections to show a cash break-even point around the end of the first year, and positive cash flow in subsequent years. You must be prepared to show the lender how you plan to handle negative cash flow. Are you seeking a loan or a line of credit to cover the entire negative cash balance? Do you also have personal resources you will be contributing? Do you have investors with available cash?

Since projections are only estimates of what will happen, it's a good idea to submit at least three projections for the same period: a worst-case scenario, a likely scenario, and a best-case scenario. Be as realistic as possible in your projections. (Many lenders will still discount your projections as too optimistic.)

If you are seeking a loan, your projections must include a "cash in" line to show the loan proceeds coming into the business. Identify how those proceeds will be spent under "cash out." Will there be equipment or inventory purchases? Don't forget to include another "cash out" line reflecting your scheduled loan payments. Your lender will look for indications that you will use the loan proceeds to generate income. He or she also will evaluate how wisely you are using cash. Obviously, your projections must demonstrate an ability to pay back the loan out of cash flow. Ask your accountant or business advisor to review your projections before you submit them.

Summing Up

Cash-flow management can be a challenge in a small business. The key to effective cash-flow management is proper planning, which will allow you to anticipate events— not just react to them. Remember: manage your business, or your business will manage you!

8

The Business of Business

ow do you make your business legal? Should you incorporate? Are you a limited partnership? In this chapter, we'll look at choosing the legal form of business that suits you best. It's important to choose one that will save you taxes and accommodate your family considerations. We'll also look at the special insurance needs of a new business, examine different types of insurance, learn how to create a plan that meets your needs, and consider some important criteria for choosing an insurance agent.

Legal Forms of Business

There are several types of business entities you may choose for your business. The most common are sole proprietorships, partnerships, and corporations. In this section, we'll examine each of these in more detail.

Sole Proprietorships

The simplest form of business is a *sole proprietorship*, which merely indicates that the business is owned and run by an individual acting alone. The owner has total control. If the owner dies or is incapacitated, the business ceases to function. The owner is solely responsible for debts and obligations of the business. Let's look at some of the advantages and disadvantages of this kind of business arrangement.

Advantages

◆ It requires the least amount of red tape to create and run.

◆ It is the least expensive to set up.

◆ You are your own boss.

Disadvantages

◆ You are completely responsible for all aspects of the business.

◆ Getting outside investments is difficult.

◆ Any debts or claims brought against the business are your *personal* responsibility.

Tax Ramifications

◆ Any profit or loss is declared on your personal income tax form.

◆ Profits generated by the business are taxable income to the owner.

◆ Profits are subject to payment of Social Security (FICA) taxes.

◆ The sole proprietor's salary is not tax-deductible because he or she is not considered an employee.

Forming a Sole Proprietorship

◆ It's very simple to form a sole proprietorship. Get a booklet from your local Secretary of State's office.

General Partnerships

A partnership is an association of two or more persons to carry on as co-owners of a business for profit. There are two kinds of partnerships. *General partners* are the people who run or manage a business. They have *unlimited liability. Limited partners* are investors who own a share of the business but don't run or manage it on a day-to-day basis. *Their liability is limited to the amount they have invested in the business.* The dissolution of a partnership may be caused by events such as the expulsion, death, bankruptcy, or withdrawal of a partner.

Advantages

◆ Partners are motivated to apply their best abilities by direct sharing of the profits.

◆ You are not alone.

Disadvantages

◆ At least one partner bears unlimited liability for the business.

◆ It is relatively difficult to obtain large sums of capital.

◆ The firm is bound by the acts of just one partner as agent.

Tax Ramifications

◆ Profits or losses are divided between the partners and are declared on their personal income tax returns.

◆ As partnerships do not pay taxes, they are merely required to file information returns.

◆ Taxation of the profit earned by the general partnership is passed through to the individual partners in proportion to each partner's distributive share of the general partnership's profit.

◆ Such income is subject to the payment of FICA taxes.

◆ Partnerships must withhold and remit FICA and unemployment insurance (FUTA) taxes.

Forming a General Partnership

◆ It is a simple process. Check with your local Secretary of State's office for instructions.

Corporations

By law, a corporation must meet all four of the following criteria: (1) It has limited liability, (2) free transferability of interests, (3) centralized management, and (4) continuity of life. A corporation is managed by a board of directors, which is elected by shareholders. The board of directors, in turn, elects officers to run the day-to-day operations of the business. Unlike other forms of business entities, a corporation continues to exist indefinitely unless it is merged with another corporation or dissolved. Interests in corporations are freely transferable, and shareholders are not personally liable for the debts and obligations of the corporation, unless the articles of incorporation provide otherwise.

In order to maintain the limited liability of shareholders, a corporation must observe the corporate formalities of keeping records, holding meetings of the shareholders and the board of directors, paying appropriate taxes, and filing required documents with the local Secretary of State, including annual reports. The failure to properly organize a corporation can subject the shareholders to personal liability. If a corporation fails to operate as a corporation, its creditors may attempt to "pierce the corporate veil" and assert claims against the shareholders personally.

Advantages

◆ Corporations have a much easier time, in general, getting investors.

◆ Corporations have a legal existence, separate from the owners or investors.

◆ If one or more of the officers or investors leaves, the business can still go on.

◆ The corporation is liable for any losses, not the individuals involved.

◆ Each person can lose only what he or she has invested.

◆ Liability is limited (but see disadvantages).

Disadvantages

◆ New corporations often cannot get credit without the owners making personal guarantees.

Tax Ramifications

◆ For a regular corporation, the taxes are paid directly by the corporation. For a Subchapter S corporation, the profits or losses are divided among the investors. Investors receive their shares of the profits or losses and declare them on their personal income taxes.

C Corporation

◆ The corporate entity pays taxes on its taxable income.

◆ If and when distributions are made to shareholders, such income is taxed at the shareholder level as well. Taxation at both the corporate and shareholder levels is known as *double taxation*.

S Corporation

◆ The corporation is not taxed on its income, but the individual shareholders are taxed on their shares of the corporation's profits, which are passed through to them.

◆ In order to qualify as an S corporation, the corporation can have no more than 35 shareholders. Only individuals, certain estates, and qualified trusts can be shareholders, and there can be no more than one class of stock.

◆ An S corporation may also not be a member of an affiliated group, which means that an S corporation may not own another corporation.

◆ An S corporation is generally not subject to state gross income tax, adjusted gross income tax, or supplemental net income tax.

Forming a Corporation

◆ Forming a corporation is more complicated than the other business forms, but it is not too difficult. You can file the necessary paperwork yourself. Pick up a booklet at your local Secretary of State's office.

What legal form will work best for your new business? In the space below, write down your answer; then list your reasons for making the choice.

_____

_____

_____

_____

Choose the Best Business Form

Now read through the following scenarios and decide which would be the best business form for each: sole proprietorship, partnership, S corporation, or C corporation.

Susan's Secretarial Service

Susan has been a legal secretary working for the same attorney for the last 10 years. He is retiring at the end of the year, so Susan must make a career move. For years she has dreamed of owning her own business, and she thinks this might be a good time to pursue that dream. She knows several people in the legal community, and she knows that most law firms have an overabundance of work. She thinks she can contract with several firms for some of their overload. She wants to work from her home and already has all of the necessary equipment to get started. What would be the best business form for her?

Movin' on Down the Road

Nicholas graduated from college six months ago and has been looking for a job ever since. He's been forced to move back home, and his parents are beginning to lose patience with him. His friend Michael spent the last five summers working for a large moving company, and now has big plans to open his own moving company. His idea is to concentrate on local moves for individuals and office moves for companies. Michael has done his homework, is sure of his market, and has convinced Nicholas to go into the business with him on a 50-50 basis. What would be the best business form for them?

Hogin, Johnson, & Associates

Darlene Hogin and Cynthia Johnson are good friends who work for a community development corporation (CDC). Darlene's main responsibility is writing proposals to government agencies and private foundations requesting funding for CDC programs and operations. Cynthia is the vice-president of operations. Darlene and Cynthia are unhappy working for their organization and decide to strike out on their own as consultants to other CDCs. With their combined skills, they're sure they will be successful. What would be the best business form for them?

Pamper Your Pet

Kathy and Mark Smith are devoted pet lovers. They both have high-paying jobs, but neither is very happy with his or her career path. They've talked about starting a family, but they can't imagine how they will care for a child since they both work such long hours.

Last Sunday, Kathy saw an ad in the paper for a pet grooming business that is for sale. She called the following morning. The owner said he would be willing to stay on until Kathy is completely trained. The price sounds fair. If Mark keeps his job and Kathy starts the new business, they can make it financially and maybe start that family. They agree to move ahead with the idea. What would be the best business form for them?

Designs by Debbie

Debbie has always considered herself an artist. She has a good computer with several graphic design programs, and she continually upgrades her equipment. She loves designing and creating all kinds of paper products. Several friends have asked her to make invitations to parties. She has even produced several wedding invitations. Sometimes her friends offer to pay her, but she doesn't feel right taking money for something she loves doing.

Recently, her friends have encouraged her to test the market, to see if there is a niche for her design business. She is reluctant, but she is tempted by the idea of making money in her own business, doing the work she loves so much. If she decides to start a business, what would be the best business form for her?

Ben's Best Brew

Ben has a beer recipe he is convinced would be a best-seller. He has tested it out on many friends, and all agree that it has a great and unusual taste. Ben has done a lot of research, and he's found that it would take about $200,000 to start producing and marketing his product. He has a well-written and thought-out business plan, and he has approached several banks, but he hasn't been able to generate any interest.

So Ben decides to approach some of his friends to see if they might be interested in buying stock in his company. He invites several friends to a Sunday brunch at his house (serving his own beer, of course) to explain the plan and ask if any of them might be interested. Although only two people say yes, Ben is convinced he'll be able to come up with enough capital to start. If he decides to start a business, what would be the best business form for him?

Insuring Your Success

As you start your business, you must consider areas for which you need insurance coverage. You don't want to insure things unnecessarily. But you also don't want to take unreasonable chances with your business.

Types of Insurance

◆ **Homeowner's or renter's insurance** protects your home and furnishings and often includes several types of protection, including fire, theft, and damage. If you plan to run your business from your home, be sure to find out if the coverage applies when your residence is used for business purposes.

◆ **Fire insurance** protects solely against fire. This may be covered by your homeowner's policy. Again, you should check to see if having a business in your home changes the coverage in any way.

◆ **Liability insurance** protects you against claims from people who are injured as a result of dealing with you or your business.

◆ **Automobile insurance** obviously covers your car. Make sure to buy liability insurance that covers injury to employees or other parties. Your current policy probably will be affected by business use.

◆ **Workers' compensation insurance** is something you must have if you have employees. It protects you and your employees in case someone is injured on the job.

◆ **Business interruption insurance** protects you if your business is forced to close unexpectedly, because of a fire or a natural disaster, for example.

◆ **Key person insurance** protects you from the loss of key personnel.

◆ **Crime insurance** protects you from outside crime, such as vandalism, break-ins, or robberies.

◆ **A blanket dishonesty bond** protects you from loss from dishonest employees.

◆ **Glass insurance** protects you from the expense of replacing broken windows.

◆ **Computer insurance** covers the cost of replacing your computer in case of fire, theft, or accidents. *(You should always have a back-up of your data!)*

◆ **Rent insurance** guarantees payment of your rent, even if your business income is interrupted by damage from weather or fire.

◆ **Employee benefits coverage:** It is unusual for a micro-business to provide employee benefits. Usually a business must employ several people before this kind of insurance is affordable. Examples of employee benefit insurance policies include group life, group health, dental, and disability.

There are other alternatives to purchasing insurance of which you should be aware. Some of the alternatives may be acceptable for your business.

◆ **Noninsurance** is ignoring the risk. This is used for all speculative risks. It is not the same as self-insurance.

◆ **Loss prevention programs** include wellness programs, safety procedures, training, and equipment such as burglar alarms and smoke detectors.

◆ **Transfer of risk** is exemplified by leasing vehicles from a company that would carry the insurance, hiring employees through temporary agencies, or drop shipping rather than storing inventory.

◆ **Self-insurance** is when you put money aside to cover possible losses.

Steps for Insurance Planning

1. **Evaluate the risks.** Think through where your business is at risk. What losses could your business not afford to cover without insurance?

2. **Set your priorities.** There will be some kinds of insurance you cannot afford to buy, and others you can afford *not* to buy. First, buy insurance for whatever could cause you the greatest loss. Remember, if you are the sole owner or a partner, anything you own personally can be taken to cover your business debts. The chance of a loss might be small, but it might also be a chance you can't afford to take. Decide which kinds of insurance you *must* have. List other kinds of insurance you would like to have. Decide which is most important.

3. **Make a plan.** Write down what insurance you need and what you want it to do for you.

4. **Find an agent.** Make sure the agent is someone you can trust. If possible, ask friends for agents they trust.

5. **Be economical.** Work with your agent to find the policy that is best for you. There are a number of ways you can get more insurance for your money, including these:

   ❧ Compare prices between companies. (Be sure you are comparing prices for the same coverage.)

   ❧ Carry as high a deductible as you can afford.

   ❧ Avoid buying insurance for something already covered in another policy.

   ❧ Buy package plans if they fit what you need.

   ❧ Buy very specific policies if you don't need more general coverage. (For example, don't pay big bucks for a renter's policy if all you want to cover is your computer.)

6. **Keep good records.** Keep complete records of all policies, including type of coverage, name of insurer, dates the coverage is effective, annual premiums, claims for losses, and amounts received. Make sure to review your coverage at least once a year. And any time there are changes that might affect your coverage, let your agent know immediately.

7. **Get expert advice.** Consult an insurance specialist who isn't trying to sell you a policy. *Be sure you have a solid plan, because you have everything to lose if you don't.* This is an area of business for which everyone should seek expert advice.

For more information on insurance, get a copy of the *Insurance Checklist for Small Business* from your local office of the Small Business Administration. (They refer to it as Management Aid #2.108.)

Choose the Right Insurance

Now read the following case studies and decide which type(s) of insurance each of these businesses *must have,* and what other type(s) of insurance they should consider.

Sam's Sod Design

Sam runs a landscaping business. He has a truck and several pieces of motorized equipment. He is the sole owner of the business, but he often employs people to help with jobs. Almost all of the work is done at job sites, but he does rent a garage to store his equipment.

Kendra's Christmas Cuties

Kendra makes hand-decorated Christmas stockings. She and a friend work out of her house. She has a couple of sewing machines and an embroidering machine. Kendra builds up stock from January through August, which she stores in her attic. She begins making deliveries of the stockings to stores early in September.

Parker's Painting

Parker is a house painter. He has an old truck, some ladders, scaffolding, and his tools. Sometimes he does jobs alone; other times, he hires one or two people to work with him. All of his work is done at the homes of his customers. If he needs to do a lot of work to prepare the walls and windows, he sets up a scaffold.

Wendy's Wordplay

Wendy is a self-employed writer. She works out of her home and has no employees. The only equipment she uses is her computer and printer, which she bought with a loan from her credit union.

Carly's Cooking

Carly runs a catering business. She and the people she hires do all of the cooking and serving. She has a small store with a large window, which she uses for displays. She also teaches a cooking class in the window, so people passing by can watch. In the back of the store she has a nicely equipped kitchen with commercial equipment.

Your Insurance Priorities

Take a few minutes to review the different kinds of insurance available to small businesses. Then, in the space below, write down which types you must have for your business.

_____

_____

_____

_____

Which other kinds of insurance would be valuable if you felt you could afford them? Check the one(s) you think are most important.

_____

_____

_____

_____

Summing Up

Take time before you start your business to decide the best form of business for you. But, if you've already started selling your product or service, don't panic. You can also change your choice of business form. Now that you are aware of your insurance needs, you should be able to find a better deal.

Managing Your Records

A well-designed system allows you to access vital information in a quick and timely manner. It's a must for your business. In this chapter, we'll review common record-keeping terms, outline how paperwork flows through a typical small business, and design a system based on that paperwork flow. Finally, at the end of the chapter you'll find important IRS guidelines for maintaining your records.

Keep Your Records Well

If your business is to succeed, you'll need a system for recording facts and maintaining records that document your daily operations.

If your system is easy to use, you are more likely to maintain it consistently. The more complicated or cumbersome the design, the more apt you are to neglect your record keeping. Below are some guidelines for effective record keeping.

Guidelines for Record Keeping

☛ Find an accountant with whom you are comfortable and create your system according to his or her directions.

☛ Make your system simple and maintain it regularly.

☛ Record business transactions only. Personal transactions must be separate from your business.

☛ Open a business checking account and use the check register to document all of your receipts (money coming in) and disbursements (money going out). Write checks to avoid making cash purchases.

☞ Save receipts to document all your business expenses.

☞ Make copies of all invoices and sales receipts issued by your business.

☞ Keep your business records for as long as the IRS recommends (usually three or four years, depending on the type of record).

☞ Store your old records in one place. Mark records according to year and record type.

☞ When you are in doubt about whether to keep a receipt or record a transaction, do! Ask your accountant later if it is correct.

Information Is a Management Tool

When you create and maintain a simple record-keeping system, you will always have the information you need at your fingertips. And make no mistake: you do need this information to manage your business wisely.

Don't drop all of your receipts and bills into a pile with the intention of getting to them later. The longer you wait, the more monumental the task becomes and the less likely you are to undertake it. It takes little effort to handle your documents correctly *as you receive them*, and it will save you a great deal of time, money, and aggravation in the long run.

Some business owners simply deliver a box stuffed with assorted documents to their accountants at the end of the year. They pay their accountants to read, sort, and record these documents, work they can easily perform themselves. Only at this point, after the fact, do they receive financial reports that tell them if their businesses are succeeding or failing. These owners manage their businesses in the dark, without the benefit of timely financial information.

A Simple System

The first step in creating a simple record-keeping system is to determine what information you need to manage your business. Different businesses have different information needs. A construction contractor might monitor labor and material expenses associated with an individual job to ensure that the expenses don't exceed the terms of the contract. A florist might track expenses by supplier or product type instead of by individual customers. A consultant may track billable hours by client. You must determine what *your* information needs are.

Next, make a list of all the paperwork you handle in your business. Include documents you receive as well as those your business generates. Then draw a diagram that shows how the paperwork flows. Once you've done this, you can design a simple method to accommodate your paperwork flow.

Common Record-Keeping Terms

☞ **Accounts payable/Trade payable:** Money you owe to your regular business creditors. Unpaid amounts are **open accounts payable.** Once they have been paid, they are **closed accounts payable**.

☞ **Accounts receivable/Trade receivable:** Money owed to you by your customers. Unpaid amounts are **open accounts receivable**. Once they have been paid, they are **closed accounts receivable**.

☞ **Cash sales:** Sales made to customers when no credit has been extended. Cash sales are paid for at the time the sale is made. Cash sales can be documented with a **cash sale invoice** or a **cash sale receipt.**

☞ **Cash receipts:** Any receipt of money. A cash receipt occurs both when a customer pays your accounts receivable (credit was extended) and when a customer pays a cash sale (no credit was extended). The term can be misleading, since it can represent cash, checks, and credit card sales.

☞ **Credit memo:** A reduction or credit applied against a previously issued invoice. Credit memos can be a result of shipping errors, price reductions, damaged goods, returns, or canceled orders. Credit memos have unique identifying numbers.

☞ **Debit memo:** An increase or debit applied against a previously issued invoice. Debit memos can be a result of original invoice errors, price adjustments, or order add-ons. Debit memos have unique identifying numbers.

☞ **Invoice:** A bill sent from a creditor to a customer. Invoices have payment terms consistent with the type of account the customer has with the creditor. Invoices have unique identifying numbers.

☞ **Invoice terms:** Payment agreement a creditor extends to a customer. Common invoice terms include these:

   🕪 **COD:** cash on delivery

   🕪 **Due upon receipt:** payment due upon receipt of invoice

   🕪 **Net 10, Net 15, Net 30:** the number of days (10, 15, 30, etc.) before payment in full is due

   🕪 **2/10 Net/30:** 2 percent discount can be taken if paid within 10 days, or full payment is due in 30 days

☞ **Packing slip:** Document a business encloses with a shipment to a customer. The packing slip verifies the contents of the shipment and compares it to the customer's order. Packing slips reference the customer's purchase order number, if applicable, and contain all relevant shipping information. Packing slips have unique identifying numbers.

☞ **Purchase order:** Form a business uses to place an order with a creditor. Purchase orders (POs) specify the buyer's name, account number, billing address, shipping address, and order details. POs have unique identifying numbers.

Fiona's Photos

Fiona is a photographer who specializes in weddings. She has just started her own business, *Fiona's Photos*. Fiona wants a record-keeping system that will keep her organized. Since she has worked for a photography studio for many years, Fiona knows what is reasonable to expect from customers and suppliers. Here is Fiona's plan:

Before she is hired to photograph a wedding, Fiona will schedule an initial consultation with the clients. During this consultation, Fiona and the clients will review samples of her work as well as her price sheet. Fiona and the clients will agree on a price based on how many rolls of film she is expected to shoot and how many hours she will remain at the wedding. Fiona will prepare a contract that both she and the clients will sign. The cost of shooting the wedding will be paid in full before the wedding date, when Fiona will give the clients a cash sale invoice (#1).

Fiona will order film from her supplier using a purchase order form. She will receive the film along with a packing slip verifying the contents of the shipment. The following week, the supplier will send an invoice for the film. After the wedding, Fiona will send the film to a photo lab so proofs can be developed. She will send a purchase order with the film so the lab knows what she wants. The lab will return the proofs with a packing slip. A week later she will receive an invoice for the proofs.

Once the proofs are developed, the clients will choose how many and what size finished photos they will purchase. Fiona will collect a 60 percent deposit from the clients before she places the final order with the photo lab. She'll give the clients another cash sale invoice (#2) for this deposit. Fiona will order the photos on a purchase order form. Once the pictures are developed, the lab will send them to Fiona with a packing slip and an invoice. Fiona will collect the 40 percent balance due from the clients when they pick up their wedding pictures. She'll make a notation on the cash sale invoice (#2) that the order has been paid in full.

Below is a list of the documents Fiona needs in her record-keeping system.

Fiona's Documents:

Type of Document	Generated By	Document Use
Customer contract	Fiona	Enter into initial agreement with client
Cash sale invoice	Fiona	Collect shooting fee from client
Purchase order	Fiona	Place order to purchase film from supplier
Packing slip	Film supplier	Delivered with film shipment to verify order
Invoice	Film supplier	Pay supplier for film
Purchase order	Fiona	Order proofs from developing lab
Packing slip	Photo lab	Delivered with proofs to verify order
Invoice	Photo lab	Pay photo lab for proofs
Cash sale invoice	Fiona	Started when 60 percent deposit is collected, and completed when 40 percent balance is collected
Purchase order	Fiona	Sent to photo lab to place picture order
Packing slip	Photo lab	Delivered with photos to verify picture order
Invoice	Photo lab	Pay photo lab for picture order

When Fiona drew a picture of her paperwork flow, it looked like this:

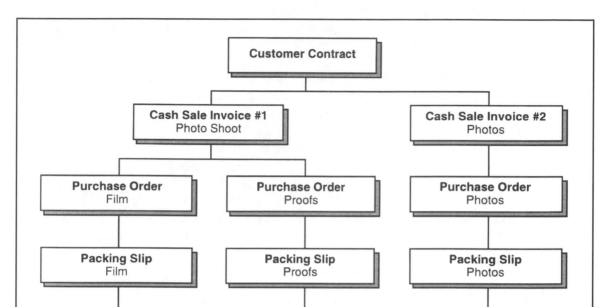

Before Fiona can organize her record-keeping system, she needs to determine what information is important to her business. For example, when Fiona accesses a client's file, she wants all the information about all the work she performed for that client. Fiona also wants to be able to pull a supplier's file and see how much business she has done with that company. She needs quick access to her outstanding accounts receivable and accounts payable balances.

Her system must be organized so that she can determine if her purchase orders were filled correctly. She will need to verify that she received a product before she pays an invoice for it. Fiona needs to organize open accounts payable so she'll know when it's time to pay a bill—not too early and not too late. She also wants to record all her transactions in one place, so that she can tell at a glance how well she is managing her money.

Here is the system Fiona designed to meet her needs:

1. **When Fiona begins working with a new client, she creates a *Client File.***
   On the file label she includes the client's name and the date the file was created. She keeps a data sheet inside the folder that includes the client's name, address, phone number, and how he or she heard about Fiona. In this folder, Fiona files the original, executed contract she and the client have both signed. She staples a few sheets of blank paper to the inside of this file folder. On this paper, she records dates and notes of conversations and meetings and all action she takes regarding this client.

2. **She creates a single file folder labeled** *Accounts Receivable Control File.* Each time Fiona issues an invoice (she uses the same numbered invoices for credit customers and cash sales), she files copy #1 here in numerical order. This is a permanent control file.

3. **If an invoice Fiona issued was for a cash sale, she stamps copy #2** *paid,* **and indicates the date, check number, and amount of payment.** She then files the paid invoice in the appropriate client file. If the invoice is not paid at the time of issue, copy #2 is filed in a single folder she has labeled *Open Accounts Receivable.* The invoice remains here until Fiona receives payment. Once it has been paid, Fiona removes the invoice from the file; marks it *paid*; records the date, check number, and payment amount; and files it in the client's file.

4. **Fiona labels a single file folder** *Purchase Orders Control File.* She keeps copy #1 of every PO she writes in this file, in numerical order. This is a permanent control file.

5. **Fiona also labels a single file folder** *Open Purchase Orders.* Each time she writes a purchase order, she files copy #2 in this file, where it remains as long as the PO is open. Each time a shipment comes in, Fiona matches the packing slip against the open purchase order. If there is a problem, Fiona calls her supplier immediately to resolve it. If there are no discrepancies, Fiona staples them together and returns them both to the *Open Purchase Orders* file.

6. **Fiona has an accordion file folder with 31 slots numbered for the days of the month.** She labels this folder *Open Accounts Payable.* Each day that she gets an invoice from a supplier, she matches the invoice against her purchase order and the packing slip (she finds these already stapled together in the *Open Purchase Orders* file). This way, she is certain she received a complete order before she pays the invoice. If everything matches, she staples the invoice to the supporting documents. Next, she checks the invoice due date. She determines the date she will need to write a check and mail it so that the payment will arrive on time. She files the invoice in *Open Accounts Payable* under the correct date. Fiona also files all other bills here, including utility, insurance, and tax bills.

   Each day, Fiona looks in the *Open Accounts Payable* file and pays the bills that are in the slot for that date. After she pays the bill, she writes the date, the check number, and amount paid on the invoice. She stamps the invoice *paid* with a red rubber stamp.

7. **Fiona has another accordion file folder, but this one has 26 slots designated A through Z.** She labels this folder *Closed Accounts Payable.* Each time Fiona pays an invoice, she files the paid invoice here, alphabetically by the creditor's name.

Below you will see a diagram of Fiona's record-keeping system. Compare it to the diagram Fiona drew earlier and you will see how Fiona's record-keeping system accommodates her natural flow of paperwork.

Fiona's Record-Keeping System

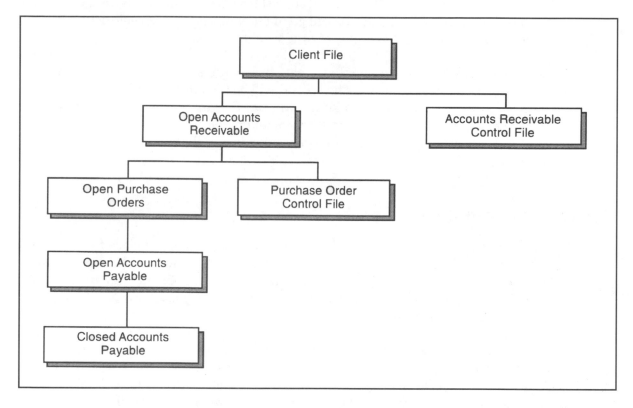

◆ Using this system, **Fiona can easily see how much money her clients owe her** by looking in the *Open Accounts Receivable* file and adding the invoice amounts.

◆ **She will always know how much money she owes her creditors** by looking in the *Open Accounts Payable* file.

◆ **She will know when her bills need to be paid,** since they are sorted by the days of the month. This will save Fiona time when she is preparing cash-flow projections each month.

◆ **Fiona can see how much she has spent with any one supplier** by looking in the *Closed Accounts Payable,* where she will find all of their paid invoices.

◆ By looking in the *Open Purchase Orders* file, **Fiona can see if she has placed any orders that have not been fulfilled.**

◆ Fiona created two control files, where invoice and PO copies are filed numerically. The control files allow her to look these up quickly by their identifying numbers. Documents in control files are never removed, so **Fiona has a permanent record of every invoice and PO her business issues.**

◆ In designing this system, Fiona has discovered that **her contract forms require at least two copies**: one for Fiona to keep in the client's file, and one to give to her clients.

◆ She learned that **her invoices will require at least three copies**. The first she will give to the customer. The second copy she will file numerically in the *Accounts Receivable Control File*. The third will go in *Open Accounts Receivable* before it is paid, then move to the *Client File* after it is paid.

◆ **Fiona's purchase orders need at least three copies**. The first will be sent to the supplier to place an order. The second will be filed numerically in the *Purchase Order Control File*. The third will begin in *Open Purchase Orders* before the order is received. Once the order has been received and invoiced, it will move to *Open Accounts Payable*. After the invoice has been paid, it will land in *Closed Accounts Payable*.

Posting to Journals

The last thing Fiona needs to add to her record-keeping system is a place to record her transactions. Businesses use *journals* to record financial transactions. Journals document events in chronological order. When a transaction has been recorded in a journal, it has been posted. A business can choose to post transactions to a *cash journal* or to a *general journal*.

In cash journals, only cash transactions are recorded. When cash sales are made and the money is deposited in the bank account, or when checks are written to pay expenses, they are recorded in the cash journal. Accounts receivable and accounts payable are *not* recorded in cash journals until they are paid. Only when cash has been received from customers or paid to creditors are the transactions recorded. Cash journals are simple to maintain, but they provide a limited amount of information.

General journals record all financial transactions—cash transactions as well as accounts receivable and accounts payable. With a general journal, a business owner can tell at a glance where money comes from, where money is going, how much money is owed to creditors, and how much money customers owe the business. A general journal gives the owner a more accurate picture of the business.

Journals should be delivered to an accountant for periodic review. The accountant can then generate financial reports quickly, which saves the business owner a great deal of money in accounting fees, since the accountant works from the journal instead of from boxes of paperwork.

Manual journals can be created using columnar pads (available in most office supply stores—see the example on the next page). If a business owns a personal computer, many computerized accounting packages are available that make record keeping easy. Journals also can be created on personal computers using spreadsheet programs.

On the following pages you will find an exercise and examples of both cash and general journals.

Columnar Pads

This is an example of a four-column columnar pad. These pads are available with 2 to 24 (or more) "currency" columns per page.

The column on the far left is used to enter the transaction date. The wide column is used to describe the transaction. The four currency columns on the right are marked so the user can easily enter dollars and cents.

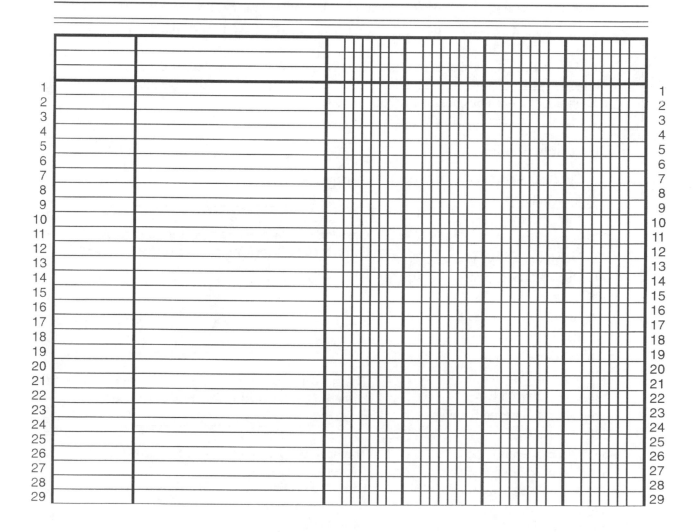

Exercise 1

In accounting, every transaction has at least two sides: one entry balanced with an equal and opposite entry. For example, when you pay the rent, you aren't just paying the rent, you disburse money from the bank to pay the rent. To record the transaction, you post one entry to the bank account and another entry to the rent expense account. Here are some examples of two sides of transactions:

	Post Entry # 1 to:	Post Entry # 2 to:
1. Make a cash sale:	Bank Account ($ deposited)	Sales Income (sale posted)
2. Pay owner's salary:	Bank Account ($ disbursed)	Salary Expense (expense posted)
3. Receive a business loan:	Bank Account ($ deposited)	Loan Payable (loan posted)

A business creates a chart of accounts to identify and number the accounts used in their accounting system. Based on the following chart of accounts, see if you can identify the "missing side" of each business transaction below.

Chart of Accounts

101 Checking Account
400 Sales Income
401 Misc. Income
500 Accounting
502 Automobile Expenses
505 Dues & Subscriptions
508 Depreciation
510 Fees: Bank Charges & Misc.
515 Insurance: Business
516 Insurance: Health
520 Interest Expense
525 Labor: Payroll Expense
526 Labor: Employee Benefits
530 Materials
545 Miscellaneous
550 Owner's Compensation
560 Repair & Maintenance
570 Taxes
580 Utilities

1. Employee health insurance premiums are paid.
    Entry 1: **516, Insurance: Health**
    (expense posted)
    Entry 2: _____

2. Gasoline expenses are reimbursed to employees.
    Entry 1: **101, Checking Account** ($ disbursed)
    Entry 2: _____

3. A customer pays cash for a purchase.
    Entry 1: **101, Checking Account** ($ deposited)
    Entry 2: _____

4. The gas bill is paid.
    Entry 1: **101, Checking Account** ($ disbursed)
    Entry 2: _____

5. The bank deducts a monthly fee directly from the checking account.
    Entry 1: **510, Fees: Bank Charges & Misc.**
    (expense posted)
    Entry 2: _____

The Cash Journal

The simplest journal to keep is a cash journal. Entries posted to this journal are based on the movement of cash in and out of the business checking account. The checkbook register is the primary source of information for a cash journal. The cash journal describes the sources of cash coming in and the uses of cash going out.

In the example that follows, column 1 is used to record transaction dates. Column 2 is used to describe each transaction. Column 3 is to record check numbers. Columns 4 and 5 are for the *Bank Account Cash In* and *Cash Out.* Next is a column for invoice numbers. Sales income is recorded in column 7. In columns 8 and 9, any other sources of cash in are posted and described. The remaining columns (10 through 16) are for commonly used operating expenses (film, proofs, photos, rent, and utilities). The last two columns are for any other cash out transactions, and expenses that don't occur often enough to require their own column.

Each time a deposit is made into the business checking account (lines 2 and 4), it is recorded in the *Bank Account Cash In,* column 4. If the source of the deposit is a sale, the sale amount is recorded in the *Sales Income*, column 7. Sometimes deposits come from other sources, such as an owner's investment or loan proceeds. These amounts are recorded in column 8 and described in column 9 (line 1).

When a check is written, it is posted in *Bank Account Cash Out,* column 5. A corresponding entry is made in the expense account columns (lines 3 and 5) or column 16, *Other Cash Out* (line 6).

At the end of the month, the columns are totaled. To determine if all entries are posted correctly, the cash journal is balanced as follows:

1. *Total Cash In* (column 4) = *Total Income* + *Other Cash In* (column 7 + 8)

2. *Total Cash Out* (column 5) = *Total Expenses* + *Other Cash Out* (columns 10 through 16)

An imbalance indicates that an entry is improperly posted or there is a mathematical error. You can perform the following calculations after the journal has been balanced:

1. Subtract *Cash Out* from *Cash In* to get the bank balance. This balance should agree with the checkbook register.

2. To determine if a profit was made or a loss sustained, subtract *Total Expenses* (columns 10 through 16) from *Total Income* (column 7).

It's easy to identify how much money is being spent in each category. Compare these to the cash-flow projections made at the beginning of the month. Is the amount of sales income as high (or higher) than projected for the month? By providing historical data, cash journal totals can be used to improve future cash-flow projections.

Fiona's Photo Studio - CASH JOURNAL

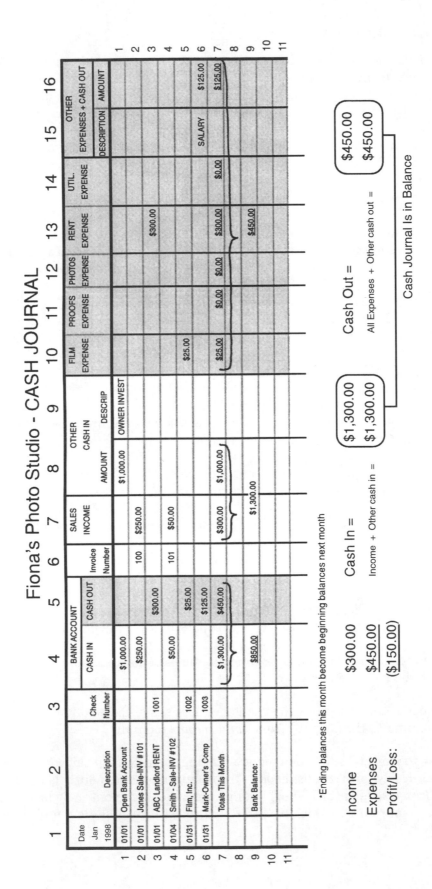

	Date Jan 1998	Description	Check Number	BANK ACCOUNT CASH IN	CASH OUT	Invoice Number	SALES INCOME	OTHER CASH IN AMOUNT	DESCRIP	FILM EXPENSE	PROOFS EXPENSE	PHOTOS EXPENSE	RENT EXPENSE	UTIL. EXPENSE	OTHER EXPENSES + CASH OUT DESCRIPTION	AMOUNT
1	01/01	Open Bank Account		$1,000.00				$1,000.00	OWNER INVEST							
2	01/01	Jones Sale-INV #101		$250.00		100	$250.00									
3	01/01	ABC Landlord RENT	1001		$300.00								$300.00			
4	01/04	Smith - Sale-INV #102		$50.00		101	$50.00									
5	01/31	Film, Inc.	1002		$25.00					$25.00						
6	01/31	Mark-Owner's Comp	1003		$125.00										SALARY	$125.00
7	01/31	Totals This Month		$1,300.00	$450.00		$300.00	$1,000.00		$25.00	$0.00	$0.00	$300.00	$0.00		$125.00
8							$1,300.00						$450.00			
9		Bank Balance:		$850.00												
10																
11																

*Ending balances this month become beginning balances next month

Income $300.00

Expenses $450.00

Profit/Loss: ($150.00)

Cash In = $1,300.00

Income + Other cash in = $1,300.00

Cash Out = $450.00

All Expenses + Other cash out = $450.00

Cash Journal Is in Balance

The General Journal

General journals require a little more work than cash journals. However, if your business has accounts receivable (A/R) and/or accounts payable (A/P), general journals give a more accurate accounting of your business.

In a general journal, A/P expenses and A/R income are recognized as they are incurred, not when they are paid. This means you post an expense when you receive an invoice, not when you pay the invoice. You post a sale when you issue the invoice to the customer, not when the customer pays the invoice.

Consider the importance of this: If your business ceased operations today, your customers would still owe you for accounts receivable issued, and you are still responsible to your creditors for accounts payable received. They reflect events that have already taken place. The general journal provides an up-to-date picture of your business because it always includes your A/R and A/P.

There is a general journal example on the next page. The general journal design is similar to the cash journal, but it includes *Accounts Receivable Issued* (column 10) and *Accounts Receivable Paid* (column 11). It also includes *Accounts Payable Received* (column 13) and *Accounts Payable Paid* (column 12).

Let's look at how A/R and A/P entries are posted to the general journal. When an invoice is issued to a customer (line 2), an entry is made under *Sales Income* (column 7) and *A/R Issued* (column 10). When the customer pays the invoice (line 7), an entry is made under *Bank Account Cash In* (column 4) and under *A/R Paid* (column 11).

When an invoice is received from a supplier (line 6), an entry is posted under *A/P Received* (column 13), and the corresponding expense account, *Film* (column 14). When the invoice is paid (line 9), an entry is made under *Bank Account Cash Out* (column 5) and under *A/P Paid* (column 12).

At the end of the month, the columns are totaled. Balancing a general journal is a little more complex than balancing a cash journal, since there are more columns. (Your accountant can help you design and balance your general journal.) These are the columns you add in this general journal to balance:

Balancing:

Bank Cash In	Bank Cash Out
A/R Issued	A/R Paid
A/P Paid	A/P Rec'd
All Expenses	Sales Income
+ Other Cash Out	+ Other Cash In
Totals =	Totals

Fiona's Photo Studio - GENERAL JOURNAL

Date Jan 1998	Description	Check #	BANK ACCOUNT CASH IN	BANK ACCOUNT CASH OUT	Invoice #	SALES INCOME AMOUNT	OTHER CASH IN AMOUNT	OTHER CASH IN DESCRIP	ACCTS RECEIVABLE ISSUED	ACCTS RECEIVABLE (PAID)	ACCTS PAYABLE PAID	ACCTS PAYABLE (RECEIVED)	FILM EXPENSE	PROOFS EXPENSE	PHOTOS EXPENSE	RENT EXPENSE	UTIL EXPENSE	OTHER EXPENSES + CASH OUT DESCRIP	OTHER EXPENSES + CASH OUT AMOUNT
01/01	Open Bank Account		$1,000.00				$1,000.00	OWNER INVEST											
01/01	Jones Sale/(A/R Issued)				100	$250.00			$250.00										
01/01	ABC Landlord (Rent)	1001		$300.00												$300.00			
01/02	Lawson Wedding				101	$100.00			$100.00										
01/04	Smith Cash Sale		$50.00		102	$50.00													
01/12	Film, Inc. (A/P Rec'd)											$25.00	$25.00						
01/15	Jones/(A/R Paid)		$250.00							$250.00									
01/16	The Photo Lab, Inc.											$415.00			$415.00				
01/31	Film, Inc. (A/P Pd.)	1002		$25.00							$25.00								
01/31	Mark - Salary	1003		$125.00														Salary	$125.00
	Totals This Month		$1,300.00	$450.00		$400.00	$1,000.00		$350.00	$250.00	$25.00	$440.00	$25.00	$0.00	$415.00	$300.00	$0.00		$125.00
	Account Balances:		$850.00						$100.00			$415.00				$865.00			

*Ending balances this month become beginning balances next month

Bank Cash In	$1,300.00	Acct Rec Balance: $100.00
Accts Receivable Issued	$350.00	Acct Pay Balance: $415.00
Accts Payables Paid	$25.00	Bank Balance: $850.00
All Expenses + Other Cash Out	$865.00	
	$2,540.00	Income: $400.00
		Expenses: $865.00
Bank Cash Out	$450.00	Profit(loss): ($465.00)
Accts Receivable Paid	$250.00	
Accts Payable Rec'd	$440.00	
All Income + Other Cash In	$1,400.00	
	$2,540.00	General Journal Is in Balance

Fiona's Photo Studio - GENERAL JOURNAL MONTH #2

			BANK ACCOUNT			SALES	OTHER CASH IN		ACCTS RECEIVABLE		ACCTS PAYABLE		FILM	PROOFS	PHOTOS	RENT	UTIL.	OTHER EXPENSES + CASH OUT	
Date Jan 1998	Description	Check #	CASH IN	CASH OUT	Invoice #	INCOME AMOUNT	AMOUNT	DESCRIP	ISSUED	(PAID)	PAID	(RECEIVED)	EXPENSE	EXPENSE	EXPENSE	EXPENSE	EXPENSE	DESCRIP	AMOUNT
1	2	3	4	5	6	7	8	9	10	11	12	13	14	15	16	17	18	19	20
	Beginning Balances:		$1,300.00	$450.00		$400.00	$1,000.00		$350.00	$250.00	$25.00	$440.00	$25.00	$0.00	$415.00	$300.00	$0.00		$125.00
02/01	ABC Landlord-RENT	1004		$300.00												$300.00			
02/01	Kennedy-Cash Sale		$150.00		103	$150.00													
02/15	Walters - (A/R Issued)				104	$400.00			$400.00										
02/28	Film, Inc.											$25.00	$25.00						
	MTD Totals:		$150.00	$300.00		$550.00	$0.00		$400.00	$0.00	$0.00	$25.00	$25.00	$0.00	$0.00	$300.00	$0.00		$0.00
	YTD Totals:		$1,450.00	$750.00		$950.00	$1,000.00		$750.00	$250.00	$25.00	$465.00	$50.00	$0.00	$415.00	$600.00	$0.00		$125.00
	YTD Acct Balances:		$700.00						$500.00			$440.00				$1,190.00			

Bank Cash In	$150.00	$1,450.00
Accts Receivable Issued	$400.00	$750.00
Accts Payables Paid	$0.00	$25.00
All Expenses + Other Cash Out	$325.00	$1,190.00
	$875.00	**$3,415.00**
Bank Cash Out	$300.00	$750.00
Accts Receivable Paid	$0.00	$250.00
Accts Payable Rec'd	$25.00	$465.00
All Income + Other Cash In	$550.00	$1,950.00
	$875.00	**$3,415.00**

Acct Rec Balance:	$500.00
Acct Pay Balance:	$440.00
Bank Balance:	$700.00
MTD Income:	$550.00
MTD Expenses:	$325.00
MTD Profit(loss):	$225.00
YTD Income:	$950.00
YTD Expenses:	$1,190.00
YTD Profit(loss):	($240.00)

General Journal Is in Balance

In the example, you can look at the totals in *A/R Issued* and *A/R Paid* and see that more invoices were issued than paid. By subtracting *A/R Paid* from *A/R Issued* you get the current outstanding *A/R Balance*: $100.

The total *A/P Received* is $440 and the total *A/P Paid* was $25. By subtracting $25 from $440, you get the current outstanding *A/P Balance*: $415.

Calculate the ending bank balance by subtracting cash out from cash in. Determine profit or loss by subtracting total expenses from sales income.

On page 107, you'll find an example of a general journal for the following month. Notice that prior month ending balances become beginning balances, and year-to-date balances are calculated.

General Information

How Long to Keep Your Records

◆ Keep all business records for at least three years from the date the tax return was due or filed, or two years from the date the tax was paid, whichever occurs later.

◆ Keep asset records that verify your basis in property for as long as they are needed to figure the basis of the original or replacement property, and/or figuring investment credit or recapture. Basis is the original cost of an item, plus additional out-of-pocket costs, such as the cost of improvements.

◆ You may need to keep some records for an indefinite period to support decisions regarding changes in accounting methods or inventory valuations.

◆ If you are an employer, retain all records and returns pertaining to employment taxes, such as income tax withholding, Social Security taxes, and federal unemployment taxes for at least four years after the due date of the return or after the date the tax was paid, whichever is later.

IRS Publication 15, *Employers Tax Guide* (Circular E) is the primary reference for an employer. Additional information and methods for special cases can be found in IRS Publication 493, *Alternative Tax Withholding Methods and Tables*.

Suggested Information Sources

IRS Publications

The following publications can be obtained through your local IRS office:

Exercise 2

Post the following transactions to the ABC Co.'s general ledger below.

☞ 2/1/98: ABC Co. makes a $25 cash sale to Mrs. Meyer.

☞ 2/2/98: Invoice #252 is issued to Mr. Klien for a $50 purchase.

☞ 2/2/98: ABC Co. receives a $30 invoice from The Office Store for file folders purchased.

☞ 2/9/98: ABC Co. writes check #101 to The Office Store for a $10 cash purchase of pencils.

☞ 2/28/98: Mr. Klien pays ABC Co. $30 against invoice #252.

Total the transactions, balance the general ledger, and fill in the blanks.

	1	2	3	4	5	6	7	8	9	10	11	12
	Date Feb 1998	Description	Check #	BANK ACCOUNT CASH IN	BANK ACCOUNT CASH OUT	Invoice #	SALES INCOME	Accts Receivable Issued	Accts Receivable Paid	Acts Payable Paid	Acts Payable Received	Off Supp EXPENSE
1		Beg. Balances:		$300.00	$145.00		$300.00	$100.00	$100.00	$145.00	$200.00	$200.00
2												
3												
4												
5												
6												
7												
8		MTD Totals:										
9												
10		YTD Totals:										
11												
12												
13		YTD Account Balances:										

YTD:

Bank Cash In
Accts Receivable Issued
Accts Payable Paid
Expenses
Total:

Bank Cash Out
Accts Receivable Pd.
Accts Payable Rec'd
Income
Total:

Is Journal in Balance?

YTD:

A/R Bal:
A/P Bal:
Bank Bal:

Income:
Expense:
Profit(Loss):

Is ABC Co. Profitable?

Publication Number	Title
15.	Employers Tax Guide (Circular E)
17.	Your Federal Income Tax
334.	Tax Guide for Small Business
463.	Travel, Entertainment, and Gift Expense
493.	Alternative Tax W/H Methods & Tables
505.	Tax Withholding & Estimated Tax
506.	Income Averaging
525.	Taxable & Nontaxable Income
533.	Self-Employment Tax
534.	Depreciation
535.	Business Expenses
539.	Employment Taxes & Information Returns
541.	Tax Information on Partnerships
542.	Tax Information on Corporations
551.	Basis for Assets
583.	Information for Business Taxpayers: Business Taxes, ID Numbers, Record Keeping
587.	Business Use of Your Home
589.	Tax Information on S Corporations
910.	Taxpayers Guide to IRS Information Assistance and Publications
	Small Business Tax Workshop Workbook

Selecting an Accountant

Here is a list of questions you should ask when you are interviewing accountants:

☛ Can you provide me with some client references from other businesses in my field?

☛ How are your fees structured?

☛ How often will we meet?

☛ What can I do to reduce your workload (and thus your fees)?

☛ Are you qualified to discuss my business's tax requirements?

☛ Will you review and advise me regarding my record keeping?

☛ What are your office hours?

☛ Is there a staff member available when you are not?

☛ How quickly will my financial reports be generated and delivered?

☛ May I have an engagement letter that details our agreement?

Employee or Independent Contractor?

According to the IRS, an employer generally must withhold income taxes, withhold and pay Social Security and Medicare taxes, and pay unemployment taxes on wages paid to an employee. An employer generally does not have to withhold or pay taxes on payments to independent contractors.

To help you determine whether an individual is an employee under the common law rules, the IRS has identified 20 factors as guidelines to determine whether sufficient control is present to establish an employer-employee relationship. These factors are only guidelines. It does not matter if you have a written agreement stating that certain factors do not apply, if the facts indicate otherwise. If an employer makes an incorrect determination and treats an employee as an independent contractor, the employer could be held personally liable for an amount equal to the taxes that should have been withheld.

To have the IRS help you determine if a worker is an employee, file Form SS-8, "Determination of Employee Work Status for Purpose of Federal Employment Taxes and Income Tax Withholding."

The 20 factors indicating whether an individual is an employee or an independent contractor are listed below:

1. **Instructions:** An employee must comply with instructions about when, where, and how to work. Even if no instructions are given, the control factor is present if the employer has a right to control how the work results are achieved.

2. **Training:** An employee may be trained to perform services in a particular manner. Independent contractors ordinarily use their own methods and receive no training from the purchaser of their services.

3. **Integration:** An employee's services usually are integrated into the business operation because the services are important to the success or continuation of the business. This shows that the employee is subject to direction and control.

4. **Services rendered personally:** An employee renders services personally. This shows the employer is interested in the methods as well as the results.

5. **Hiring assistants:** An employee works for an employer who hires, supervises, and pays workers. An independent contractor can hire, supervise, and pay assistants under a contract that requires him or her to provide materials and labor and to be responsible only for the results.

6. **Continuing relationship:** An employee generally has a continuing relationship with an employer. A continuing relationship may exist even if work is performed at recurring, irregular intervals.

7. **Set hours of work:** An employee usually has set hours of work established by an employer. An independent contractor generally can set his or her own hours.

8. **Full-time required:** An employee may be required to work or to be available full-time. This indicates control by the employer. An independent contractor can work when and for whom he or she chooses.

9. **Work done on premises:** An employee usually works on the premises of an employer, or works on a route or at a location designated by the employer.

10. **Order or sequence set:** An employee may be required to perform services in the order or sequence set by an employer. This shows the employee is subject to direction and control.

11. **Reports:** An employee may be required to submit reports to an employer. This shows the employer maintains a degree of control.

12. **Payments:** An employee is paid by the hour, week, or month. An independent contractor usually is paid by the job or on a straight commission.

13. **Expenses:** An employee's business and travel expenses generally are paid by an employer. This shows the employee is subject to regulation and control.

14. **Tools and materials:** An employee usually is furnished significant tools, materials, and other equipment by an employer.

15. **Investment:** An independent contractor has a significant investment in the facilities he or she uses in performing services for someone else.

16. **Profit or loss:** An independent contractor can make a profit or suffer a loss.

17. **Works for more than one person or firm:** An independent contractor generally is free to provide his or her services to two or more unrelated persons or firms at the same time.

18. **Offers services to the general public:** An independent contractor makes his or her services available to the general public.

19. **Right to fire:** An employee can be fired by an employer. An independent contractor cannot be fired so long as he or she produces a result that meets the specifications of the contract.

20. **Right to quit:** An employee can quit his or her job at any time without incurring liability. An independent contractor usually agrees to complete a specific job and is responsible for its satisfactory completion, or is legally obligated to make good for failure to complete it.

Remember, these factors should be considered only as guidelines. Not every factor applies in every situation, and the degree of importance of each factor varies, depending on the type of work and individual circumstances. However, all relevant factors are considered in making a determination, and no one factor is decisive.

Summing Up

An effective record-keeping system is a must for your small business. A well-designed system is simple and easy to use, and allows you to access important information quickly. Consider what information you need to manage your business, what paperwork your business generates, and what documents you receive as you design your system. Don't be afraid to consult a bookkeeper or an accountant familiar with your type of business to assist you in setting up your system.

10

Understanding Financial Statements

In this chapter, we'll learn to read financial statements. Successful business owners use financial reports as vital management tools. Most small businesses don't generate their own financials, but all small business owners should understand how to read them.

Once you understand the components of financial statements, you'll have the chance to examine the effect different management decisions have on similar businesses. You'll also learn what lenders look for when analyzing financial reports.

Just the Facts, Ma'am

Who?

Financial statements are used by many people, but none more important than the business owner. Successful business owners use financial statements as management tools. They refer to these reports on a regular basis to make daily operating decisions. And before they make any critical business decision, they examine their financial reports.

Some business owners believe that financial statements are for accountants and bankers. They pay an accountant to generate the statements and then send copies to the bank. They rely on their accountant to read the reports and alert them to any problems. By doing this, they relinquish some control of their businesses and rely on chance that everything will be all right.

What?

Financial statements consist of two primary elements: the balance sheet and the income statement. When people ask for financial statements, sometimes they also want other reports, such as cash-flow statements or projections.

When?

How often financial statements should be generated and reviewed depends on the size and type of business. Some businesses need only quarterly financial reports, but most businesses are better served with monthly reports. If your record-keeping system includes an up-to-date general journal, you'll already have considerable financial information on a daily basis. Your accountant can help you determine what best suits your information needs.

Why?

Operating a business without financial statements is like driving a car blindfolded. You wouldn't know when (or if) you reached your destination—and that would be the least of your problems. More important, you couldn't see obstacles in your way, and you wouldn't know if you were in danger until it was too late. You couldn't see what you were doing right or where you were going off course. You could get hurt because of your recklessness, and so could others. Driving blindfolded is not smart. Whether driving a car or running a business, you need to see where you've been, where you are, and where you're going.

Before you can use your financial statement as a management tool, you must first understand how to read it.

You Ought to Be in Pictures!

Financial statements are pictures of your business that serve two important functions:

1. The balance sheet reports the net worth of the business.

2. The income statement reports how the business is being operated.

The Balance Sheet

The balance sheet is a financial snapshot of your business at a given point in time. It tells you, as of a specific date, several important things:

☞ What your business owns

☞ The debt for which your business is liable

☞ And the net worth of your business

The information is categorized as follows:

☞ Assets (what you own)

☞ Liabilities (what you owe)

☞ Equity (your net worth)

Since a balance sheet is a financial picture taken on a specific date, it is labeled as such: Balance sheet for ABC Company, Inc., as of XX/XX/XXXX

The Income Statement

Your income statement is a "financial movie" that covers a specific period of time. It tells you if your business operated at a profit or suffered a loss during a specific period of time.

This information is categorized as follows:

☞ Income (revenue generated)

☞ Expenses (cost of operations)

☞ Profit or loss (difference between income and expenses)

Since an income statement covers a specific period, it is labeled as such: Income Statement for ABC Company, Inc., for the period ending XX/XX/XXXX

Exercise 1

Perhaps the easiest way to understand financial statements is to examine a set. In this exercise, we'll identify an asset, liability, equity, income, and expense item, and indicate whether each is found on the balance sheet or income statement.

Month # 1	Description	Balance Sheet/ Income Statement
Mary's take-home pay from her job is $2,000 per month.	Income	Income Statement
Her living expenses total $1,500 per month.	Expenses	Income Statement
The difference between her income and expense is $500.	Profit (Loss)	Income Statement
Mary puts her monthly "profit" into a savings account.	Asset	Balance Sheet
Mary just bought a car for $6,000.	Asset	Balance Sheet
She put $1,000 down to buy the car.	Equity	Balance Sheet
Mary has an auto loan with a balance of $5,000.	Liability	Balance Sheet
Mary is buying a house; the purchase price is $45,000.	Asset	Balance Sheet
She put $5,000 down on the house.	Equity	Balance Sheet
She has a mortgage loan balance of $40,000.	Liability	Balance Sheet

Mary's Balance Sheet as of 1/31/98

Assets		Liabilities	
Bank Balance	$500	Mortgage loan	$40,000
House	$45,000	Car loan	$5,000
Car	$6,000	**Liabilities:**	**$45,000**
Assets:	**$51,500**		
		Equity (net worth)	
		Home equity:	$5,000
		Car equity:	$1,000
		Profit (Loss)	$500
		Equity:	**$ 6,500**
Total Assets:	**$51,500**	**Total Liabilities & Equity:**	**$51,500**

Mary's Income Statement as of 1/31/98

Income
Salary	$2,000

Expenses
Mortgage Payment	$ 500
Food	200
Utilities	300
Insurance	100
Auto Payment	300
Miscellaneous	100
Total Expenses	**$1,500**
Profit (Loss)	**$ 500**

Is This Picture in Focus?

Let's take a closer look at examples of *assets*, *liabilities*, and *equity*:

◆ David buys a car for $5,000. He puts $1,000 down and takes out a car loan for $4,000.

Asset (what you own)	Automobile	$5,000
Liability (what you owe)	Auto loan	$4,000
Equity (net worth)	Auto equity	$1,000

◆ Kathy buys a house for $40,000. Her down payment is $5,000. Her mortgage is $35,000.

Asset (what you own)	Home	$40,000
Liability (what you owe)	Mortgage	$35,000
Equity (net worth)	Home equity	$5,000

◆ James has a savings account balance of $2,000. He has credit card debt of $1,800.

Asset (what you own)	Savings account	$2,000
Liability (what you owe)	Credit card debt	$1,800
Equity (net worth)	Net worth	$200

Looking at the examples above, you will notice that there is a common equation:

Assets – Liabilities = Equity

Another way to write this same equation is as follows:

Assets = Liabilities + Equity

Let's test this and see if it works.

	Assets – Liabilities = Equity	*or*	**Assets = Liabilities + Equity**
David:	$5,000 – $4,000 = $1,000	*or*	$5,000 = $4,000 + $1,000
Kathy:	$40,000 – $35,000 = $5,000	*or*	$40,000 = $35,000 + $5,000
James:	$2,000 – $1,800 = $200	*or*	$2,000 = $1,800 + $200

Assets = Liabilities + Equity is *the* fundamental accounting equation. Balance sheets are so called because they are designed to balance using this equation. Following is an example of a balance sheet.

David's Balance Sheet as of 1/31/98

Assets		Liabilities	
Automobile	$5,000	Auto loan	$4,000
		Equity	
		Auto equity	$1,000
Total Assets:	**$5,000**	**Total Liabilities & Equity:**	**$5,000**

The Whole Family Album

Income statements describe operating income and expenses over a period of time (for example, one month). If a business generates more income than expense, it earns a profit. If a business incurs more expense than income, it suffers a loss.

We know that balance sheets report the net worth (equity) of a business and that income statements report profit or loss. If a business is profitable, doesn't that increase its equity? If a business is suffering a loss, doesn't that decrease it's equity? If so, then doesn't the profit or loss of the income statement need to be reflected on the balance sheet?

The answer is yes. Profit or loss is taken directly from the income statement and recorded on the balance sheet in an equity account called *retained earnings*. In the following example, we'll see how this happens.

ABC Widgets

ABC Widgets is owned by Mr. I. M. Good. Mr. Good started his business with an initial investment of $5,000.

Here is Mr. Good's opening balance sheet:

Balance Sheet for ABC Widgets as of 1/1/98

Assets		Liabilities	
Bank account	$5,000	Accounts payable	$0
Accounts receivable	$0		
Inventory	$0	**Equity**	
Equipment	$0	Owner's equity	$5,000
		Retained earnings	$0
		Total Equity	**$5,000**
Total Assets	**$5,000**	**Liabilities & Equity**	**$5,000**

Mr. Good started his business with $5,000 of his personal savings. His investment in his business is recorded as *equity* in an account called *owner's equity*. The $5,000 balance will remain unless Mr. Good reduces or increases his investment into his business. Mr. Good deposited the cash in the *bank account*. The opening balance sheet is in balance.

Mr. Good decided to market his new business aggressively. His decision to spend money on advertising has paid off. Sales are above Mr. Good's projections, and he has made a net profit of $570. Here is Mr. Good's first income statement:

Mr. Good collected $4,700 in widget sales. That income was deposited into the bank account. He also paid $1,645 in COGS, and $2,485 in fixed expenses. By the end of the month, his bank balance was $5,570. The balance sheet reflects this new bank balance.

ABC Widgets earned a profit of $570. This amount is recorded as *equity, retained earnings*.

Below is the balance sheet at the end of the month:

Income Statement for ABC Widgets for Month Ending 1/31/98

Income	
Widget sales	$4,700
Total Sales	**$4,700**
Cost of Goods Sold	
Widget material	$705
Widget labor	$940
Total Cost of Goods Sold	**$1,645**
Gross Profit	**$3,055**
Fixed Expenses	
Advertising	$1,000
Automobile	$100
Bank charges	$10
Insurance	$100
Office supplies	$25
Owner's compensation	$750
Rent	$500
Total Fixed Expenses	**$2,485**
Net Profit	**$570**

Balance Sheet for ABC Widgets as of 1/31/98

Assets		Liabilities	
Bank account	$5,570	Accounts payable	$0
Accounts receivable	$0		
Inventory	$0	**Equity**	
Equipment	$0	Owner's equity	$5,000
		Retained earnings	$570
		Total Equity	**$5,570**
Total Assets	**$5,570**	**Liabilities & Earnings**	**$5,570**

XYZ Gadgets

I. M. Good's Brother, Notso, started a business the same month: XYZ Gadgets. Notso also started with a $5,000 investment. Notso's opening balance sheet for XYZ was identical to ABC's balance sheet.

Notso made some different management decisions. He spent very little time and money marketing his new business; as a result, his sales are less than he had hoped for. He had to pay high prices for materials because he didn't take advantage of volume discounts. His labor costs were high because he didn't hire experienced employees; the inexperienced staff was slow in producing gadgets. Notso didn't pay himself a salary. He ended the month with a $10 loss.

Income Statement for XZY Gadgets for Month Ending 1/31/98

Income

Gadget sales	$1,500
Total Sales	**$1,500**

Cost of Goods Sold

Gadget material	$300
Gadget labor	$375
Total Cost of Goods Sold	**$675**
Gross Profit	**$825**

Fixed Expenses

Advertising	$100
Automobile	$100
Bank charges	$10
Insurance	$100
Office supplies	$25
Owner's compensation	$0
Rent	$500
Total Fixed Expenses	**$835**
Net Profit	**($10)**

During the month, Notso collected $1,500 in cash sales, paid $675 in COGS, and $835 in fixed expenses. His ending bank balance was $4,990.

Notso posted a loss of $10.00 to retained earnings.

Balance Sheet for XYZ Gadgets as of 1/31/98

Assets

Bank account	$4,990
Accounts receivable	$0
Inventory	$0
Equipment	$0
Total Assets	**$4,990**

Liabilities

Accounts payable	$0

Equity

Owner's equity	$5,000
Retained earnings:	($10)
Total Equity	**$4,990**
Liabilities & Equity	**$4,990**

I. M. and Notso started their businesses on the same day with the same amount of money. In one month, ABC was earning a profit, but XYZ was suffering a loss. Is XYZ worth less than ABC?

Cash vs. Credit

In the prior examples, ABC's transactions were all made in cash: Cash sales were deposited into the bank account, and cash expenses were paid from the bank account. Here's what that balance sheet looked like:

Balance Sheet for ABC Widgets as of 1/31/98

Assets		Liabilities	
Bank account	$5,570	Accounts payable	$0
Accounts receivable	$0		
Inventory	$0	**Equity**	
Equipment	$0	Owner's equity	$5,000
		Retained earnings	$570
		Total Equity	**$5,570**
Total Assets	**$5,570**	**Liabilities & Equity**	**$5,570**

Let's see what would happen if ABC had the *same amount of sales and expenses*, but incurred accounts receivable for some of those sales and accounts payable for some of those expenses.

◆ Remember, sales totaled $4,700. Let's assume that $4,000 was paid in cash, and $700 remained in A/R.

◆ Expenses (COGS & fixed) totaled $4,130. Let's assume that $3,000 was paid in cash, and $1,130 remained in A/P.

◆ The bank account had $5,000 in cash at the beginning of the month. Add $4,000 in cash sales, and subtract $3,000 in expenses paid. The ending bank balance is $6,000.

◆ The accounts receivable balance is $700. The accounts payable balance is $1,130.

◆ The income statement reflects no changes, and retained earnings are still $570.

The new balance sheet would look like this:

Balance Sheet for ABC Widget as of 1/31/98

Assets		Liabilities	
Bank account	$6,000	Accounts payable	$1,130
Accounts receivable	$700		
Inventory	$0	**Equity**	
Equipment	$0	Owner's equity	$5,000
		Retained earnings	$570
		Total Equity	**$5,570**
Total Assets	**$6,700**	**Liabilities & Equity**	**$6,700**

The business has increased assets and increased liabilities; but the *equity* of the business did not change.

The Chart of Accounts

In a business, transactions occur daily. For ease in identifying all of the accounts a business may use, a listing or *chart of accounts* is created. These accounts often are numbered for easy identification. If you created a personal chart of accounts, it might look like this:

Assets
100 Bank Account
110 House
120 Car

Liabilities
200 Home Mortgage
210 Auto Loan

Equity
300 Home Equity
310 Auto Equity
333 Profit (Loss)

Income
400 Salary Income

Expenses
510 Mortgage Payment
520 Food
530 Utilities
540 Insurance
550 Auto Payment
560 Miscellaneous

Companies create their own charts of accounts, relative to the way they do business. Throughout the year, they can add new accounts to their charts as necessary. An accountant or bookkeeper can help a business establish a chart of accounts that meets its needs. A simple chart of accounts follows:

Assets
100 Regular Checking Account
105 Payroll Checking Account
110 Petty Cash on Hand
115 Trade Accounts Receivable
150 Equipment
155 Furniture and Fixtures
160 Small Tools
180 Inventory on Hand

Liabilities
200 Trade Accounts Payable
205 Payroll Taxes Payable
210 Bank Note Payable
250 Note Payable: Owner

Equity
300 Owner's Contribution
399 Retained Earnings: Year to Date

Income
400 Sales Income
401 Misc. Income

Expenses
500 Accounting
502 Automobile Expense
505 Dues and Subscriptions
508 Depreciation
510 Fees: Bank Charges & Misc.
515 Insurance: Business
516 Insurance: Health
520 Interest Expense
525 Labor: Payroll Expense
526 Labor: Employee Benefits
530 Materials
545 Miscellaneous
550 Owner's Compensation
560 Repair & Maint.
570 Taxes
580 Utilities

A Picture in Review

Let's review what we've learned so far. There are five types of accounts:

1. Assets (what you own)

2. Liabilities (what you owe)

3. Equity (net worth)

4. Income

5. Expenses

Balance Sheet

Assets	Liabilities
	Equity

Assets = Liabilities + Equity

☞ Contains assets, liabilities, and equity

☞ Reports net worth as of a specific date

☞ Must balance

Income Statement

Income
− Expenses

= Net Profit (Loss)

☞ Contains income and expenses

☞ Reports operating profit or loss for a specific period of time

If a business earns a profit, equity increases.

If a business suffers a loss, equity decreases.

Profit or loss is posted to the balance sheet in an equity account called retained earnings.

Retained Earnings Accumulate

You know there is a relationship between income statements and balance sheets: Profit or loss from the income statement is posted to the balance sheet as retained earnings. In the first month of operations, profit or loss and retained earnings will be the same. Each month thereafter, the profit or loss amount from the monthly income statement is added to the prior retained earnings balance.

Exercise 2

In this exercise, you will create financial statements. Fill in the blanks; then enter the information onto the worksheet on the following page.

1. The name of your imaginary person is _____. Enter this name at the top of both the balance sheet and the income statement.

2. Your person brings home a salary of $_____ each month. Enter this amount on the income statement. If your person has other income, identify this also.

3. Your person is buying a _____. The purchase price is $_____(asset) and is being purchased with a down payment of $_____ (equity) and a loan for the balance of $_____(liability). Enter these amounts on the balance sheet.

4. The monthly household expenses for your person are the following:

Housing expense	$ _____
Food	_____
Utilities	_____
Insurance	_____
Car payment	_____
Daycare	_____
_____	_____
_____	_____
_____	_____
_____	_____
_____	_____

    Enter these amounts where they belong on the income statement.

5. If you'd like, your person is also purchasing a _____ . The purchase price is $_____ and is being purchased with a down payment of $_____ and a loan for the balance of $_____. Enter these amounts on the balance sheet. If your person owns anything else, or owes anything else, include these amounts also.

6. Total your income statement and determine if your person ends with a profit or loss. Remember to reflect this amount on the balance sheet.

7. Now total your balance sheet. Remember that *the balance sheet must balance.* If it doesn't, try to determine what is missing.

    HINT: Did your person end with a profit or loss in number 6? Where did that cash go— into a checking account? Did you remember to include a checking account on the balance sheet?

Exercise 2 Worksheet

_____

Balance Sheet as of 1/31/98

Assets

_____ $_____

_____ $_____

_____ $_____

_____ $_____

Liabilities

_____ $_____

_____ $_____

_____ $_____

_____ $_____

Equity (net worth)

_____ $_____

_____ $_____

_____ $_____

Total Assets $_____   Liabilities & Equity $_____

_____

Income Statement for Period Ending 1/31/98

Income

_____ $_____

_____ $_____

_____ $_____

Expenses

_____ $_____

_____ $_____

_____ $_____

_____ $_____

_____ $_____

_____ $_____

_____ $_____

_____ $_____

Profit (Loss) $_____

Summing Up

The following are typical questions lenders and accountants ask when analyzing financial statements. Keep them in mind when you review your own:

1. Do assets exceed liabilities? Is there a positive or negative net worth?

2. Does it appear that the values assigned to the assets are reasonable? Assets are posted at their purchase price and adjusted to market price as necessary. Have reasonable adjustments been made? Do adjustments need to be made?

3. Are the assets things that can be sold quickly if necessary? What type of assets are they? How well do they hold their value?

4. Do assets exceed liabilities by a large margin? If some assets had to be sold (liquidated) to pay debts, what would remain?

5. Comparing income to expenses and liabilities, does it seem that money is being spent well?

6. If the company suffered a sudden reduction or fluctuation in income, are there monthly expenses that could be reduced or eliminated easily?

7. Are there large swings in expenses that do not correspond to swings in sales? Does it appear that the company is not controlling operating expenses?

8. Do accounts receivable greatly exceed an average month of sales? If so, chances are good that receivables are not being collected in a timely manner. The older receivables become, the more difficult they are to collect.

9. Do accounts payable greatly exceed an average month of operating expenses? If so, chances are good that bills are not being paid on time. This could result in suppliers no longer extending credit or delivering goods, utilities being disconnected, and loans being called.

10. Are there unexplained accounts payable, such as loans or notes?

11. How much money does the owner have invested in the business? How does this compare to overall debt? Is the company being operated using nothing but OPM (other people's money)?

12. How much salary is the owner taking out of the business? How does this compare to the profit or loss of the business?

Financial statements are excellent management tools. Learn to understand them and use them.

From Dream to Reality

Turning your self-employment dream into reality can be both exhilarating and a bit frightening. This book was written to take some of the mystery out of the process of starting your own business. In this book, we've looked at some of the reasons people decide to become self-employed, and why some businesses fail. We've helped you define your dream and understand how to finance it. We've shown you how to set goals and create action plans to achieve them. We've given you the worksheets to price your products and services, and the steps to market your business. We've provided information about legal forms of business, insurance, cash-flow management, record keeping, and financial statements.

Each chapter for this book gives you information about a different aspect of your small business. Consider each aspect and how it applies to your business idea. As you plan your business, step-by-step, write down your ideas. This will become your business plan—your personal guide to starting your own business. Your business plan will help keep you grounded as your dream becomes a reality. Use it to communicate your ideas to other people. As your business grows, your business plan should be reviewed and updated to accommodate changes.

Self-employment has many rewards; among them is the satisfaction of having a dream and turning it into something real. Good luck on your journey from dream to reality.

Business Plan

Cathy's Cleaning Service, Inc.

Cathy Smith, President
P.O. Box 2927
Indianapolis, IN 46206
(317) 000-0000

Table of Contents

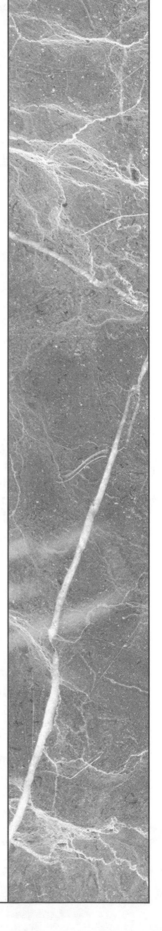

Cathy's Cleaning Service, Inc.
Business Plan

Introduction

Description of Business

Cathy's Cleaning Service, Inc. (CCSI), is a full-service residential and commercial cleaning company. The business has been owned and operated by Cathy Smith since June 1992, and is a Sub-S Corporation, incorporated in June 1993. The business office is located at 01 N. America's Avenue, Suite 350, Indianapolis, IN 46201. The business phone number is (317) 000-0000.

In June 1992, Cathy Smith was a mother of two school-age children and a full-time homemaker when she began cleaning homes for neighbors. Within six months, Cathy was regularly cleaning two residences and had one commercial property contract. She hired her mother and two sisters as part-time employees and has since added to her staff.

Currently, CCSI has three full-time and four part-time employees who work in teams to provide services to clients. Two of the full-time employees and three part-time employees make up the commercial cleaning department, and the remaining employees operate in the residential cleaning department. Commercial contracts are awarded annually, and residential cleaning is done on an ongoing basis unless a homeowner wishes to make a change.

The business goal of CCSI is to provide high-quality residential and commercial cleaning services to customers at a reasonable price, which will allow the corporation and its owners to recognize a profit. It is also the mission of the company to foster a healthy working environment, to pay competitive and fair wages to its employees, and to encourage employees to develop a healthy balance between work and family commitments.

The company owner recently completed taking a business planning course to improve her ability to analyze and monitor pricing and produce long- and short-term cash-flow projections. Additionally, it is the intention to send the owner and one manager to a personnel management course. A short-term capital equipment loan is required to add industrial vacuums and other cleaning equipment, thereby allowing the firm to grow by taking on more commercial contracts.

Marketing

Service Description

CCSI offers residential and light commercial cleaning. For residential customers, each job is bid according to the size of the home, the number of individuals residing in the home, and the scope of services required. There are three service packages from which the homeowner will be able to choose. These are outlined below:

◆ Residential Cleaning # 1 — Frequency of visits: 1–4 times per month
Includes: dusting of all surfaces, vacuuming all carpeted areas, sweeping and mopping all vinyl or tile floor areas, complete bathroom cleaning, loading dirty dishes into a dishwasher (no hand washing dishes), up to three full loads of laundry washed, dried, folded, and stacked, general light housecleaning.

◆ Residential Cleaning # 2 — Frequency of visits: 1–4 times per month
Includes: dusting of all surfaces, vacuuming all carpeted areas, sweeping and mopping all vinyl or tile floor areas, complete bathroom cleaning, general light housecleaning.

◆ Residential Cleaning # 3 — Frequency of visits: One-time cleaning
Includes all of the services offered in package #1, plus window washing (inside only), and oven cleaning. This cost of this package is an actual per-hour cost of $10.00 per hour per cleaning person.

The most commonly purchased residential package is #1. Package #2 is usually ordered by the single customer or the customer who may not work full-time outside of the home. Package #3 is most often ordered for special occasions, such as weddings or family reunions.

Custom packages are available for customers who have special needs.

Commercial cleaning is bid on a custom basis. The owners or property managers of a commercial building will meet with the owner of CCSI and decide on the frequency of visits and services to be offered. Commonly, the services performed in commercial buildings include emptying trash and ash receptacles, vacuuming carpeted areas, damp mopping vinyl and tile floor areas, and cleaning rest rooms. The professional cleaners of CCSI will not remove or disturb anything atop desks or other personal work areas. Work surfaces, computers, and other electronic equipment will be lightly dusted but not disturbed. All bids for services will be prepared by Cathy Smith.

Market Description

CCSI is located on the near East side of Indianapolis. The target markets for cleaning services are the residential and commercial customers located on the East and near East sides of Indianapolis.

The primary residential target customers are families in which both parents are employed outside the home and have two or more children. According to *American Demographic* magazine, 43 percent of families of four or larger, in which both parents are employed outside the home utilize a professional housecleaning service at least once a month. Of that 43 percent, 51 percent prefer to use a local, privately-owned service as opposed to a franchise operation. They state the reasons for this preference are more dependable service, greater ability to customize services, and more flexible working agreements.

The second target market for residential customers is the single executive. *American Demographic* magazine finds that 37 percent of singles earning an annual income of $40,000 or greater utilize a cleaning service at least one time per month.

According to the 1990 census report for Indianapolis, 22 percent of all metropolitan Indianapolis families of four or larger in which both parents are working outside the home live in the near East side and the East side neighborhoods of Indianapolis. Only 7 percent of the single executives earning annual incomes of $40,000 or greater reside in this same geographic area.

The commercial market CCSI targets are the small office buildings that employ 50 or fewer employees. Larger offices tend to utilize large, franchise cleaning services, and very large, multibusiness office buildings often have on-staff cleaning services. Industrial buildings are often quite difficult and time-consuming to clean and are not included in the target market for CCSI.

According to the *Commercial Real Estate Update* (local) magazine, the near East side of Indianapolis contains over 30 percent of all small commercial office buildings in the downtown or near downtown areas.

Competition

As of December 31, 1993, there were only two privately-owned cleaning services and no franchise services that specifically serviced this geographic area of Indianapolis. Comparatively, there are 27 privately-owned services and four large franchise services that target the North, Northwest, and Northeast areas of metropolitan Indianapolis. The South, Southeast, and Southwest areas are serviced by another 15 companies, and the West side of town is targeted by another 12 companies. Even though the East and near East side neighborhoods do not make up the larger portion of the target residential customer, the lack of existing competition and the existing contacts CCSI has established make this a very good market in which to sell its services. The facts that CCSI has an office located in the near East side and that all of its employees live in the East side allow CCSI to be more responsive to customer needs.

Most commercial cleaning services prefer to bid on the multioffice, larger office buildings, and a survey conducted by CCSI mailed to local office buildings found that the smaller buildings have had difficulty finding services willing to clean their offices.

CCSI offers service to an area that is poorly serviced at this time. CCSI also offers custom cleaning services, tailored to the specific size of each location and the services requested by the individual customer—something the larger franchise firms do not offer. For residential and commercial customers alike, the fact that CCSI has established a reputation for honest, dependable cleaning people is quite attractive. All employees are bonded, and a police background check is performed prior to hire to ensure high-quality employees. Supervisors are assigned to monitor work crews, thereby providing added security for the customer.

Marketing Strategy

CCSI markets its cleaning services through advertisements in the local *Near Eastside Neighbor* and *INDY East* newspapers. Additionally, five local church bulletins are used to advertise services. Fliers are posted at four local beauty shops, one local grocery store, and two service stations. A referral program is being offered to existing customers whereby an existing customer who refers a new customer gets a $25 discount on future cleaning services.

Through a local property management company, which manages seventy single-family rental units, one free housecleaning will be awarded (program to begin next month) to a resident who wins this service in a semiannual drawing (all residents who pay their rent early or on time for six months in a row are eligible for the drawing). In the commercial buildings CCSI cleans, one free residential cleaning will be awarded per year to each customer, to be given away as the commercial building owner/manager wishes (such as to employees as an "employee of the year" award). Also, cleaning gift certificates for $25, $50, and $75 will be offered to commercial accounts as gifts for employees or preferred customers. Of course, these gift certificates will also be available to residential customers. Once every quarter, all residential and commercial customers will receive a newsletter outlining all current marketing programs.

Word-of-mouth advertising still remains the most effective method of growth for CCSI. All customer suggestions are responded to in writing, and all phone calls are returned within 24 hours. By paying special attention to all customers, and frequently (at least once a quarter) contacting all customers by telephone or in person to see if they remain satisfied with the level of services offered, CCSI continues to build a loyal clientele.

Organization

Quality Control

CCSI recognizes the importance of delivering high-quality service in order to maintain a loyal customer base. In order to ensure that cleaning is done to the high standards of CCSI, supervisors regularly inspect the work performed. For residential customers who contract CCSI to clean regularly, at least one cleaning per month is supervised by a manager. For residential customers who contract a single or special-event cleaning, every work crew is headed by a manager who supervises the cleaning. Every commercial work crew is accompanied by a manager who supervises the cleaning of office buildings.

Work crews are scheduled weekly. Two full-time and three part-time employees are regularly scheduled to perform on the commercial contracts. One full-time and one part-time employee regularly clean residential properties. Cathy Smith regularly accompanies work crews as a supervisor. Each work crew has a checklist that must be reviewed before leaving the work site. The checklist ensures that all services contracted are actually performed. The crew leader signs the checklist and becomes responsible for any discrepancies reported by the customer. All cleaning products are provided by CCSI unless a customer specifically requests that a certain product be used. This ensures consistent use of high-quality cleaning products.

Since CCSI contacts every customer at least once each quarter, it allows customers to voice any concerns or complaints they may have regarding the quality of work performed. Customer suggestions are always considered and implemented whenever possible.

Legal Structure

CCSI is a Sub-S Corporation, incorporated in June, 1993. The business is operated by the sole owner, Cathy Smith. CCSI originally started doing business in 1992 as a sole proprietorship and converted to a Sub-S for limited liability protection.

Insurance

CCSI carries business liability insurance through Mr. Allen Green of the ABC Insurance Agency. The insurance Underwriter is AmerInsurance.

Additionally, all employees of CCSI are bonded. Workmens' Compensation and a life insurance policy on Cathy Smith are also sold to CCSI by the same agency.

Management

Cathy Smith is the President and General Manager of CCSI. Her background includes supervisory positions for over 10 years, managing as many as 15 employees in a manufacturing environment. Cathy left the job market for 10 years when she married and had two children, and began CCSI when her youngest child started first grade.

Cathy hires and trains employees, schedules residential and commercial cleaning, purchases supplies, negotiates contracts, markets the company, and manages all accounts receivable and payable. Each cleaning crew has a crew leader who immediately supervises all work, and each division has a manager who takes responsibility for supervising the crew leaders. Additionally, Cathy acts as a manager in both divisions.

The manager in the commercial cleaning division, Sarah Jones, has five years of experience working as a manager for a national franchise cleaning service. Sarah has worked for CCSI since October, 1992.

The residential cleaning division manager, Mary Murphy, has two years of experience as the head of housekeeping services for a large, local hotel. Mary has been employed with CCSI since January, 1993.

Cathy maintains accounts receivable and payable for CCSI. She collects all business-related receipts and maintains the company checkbook and other records. On a quarterly schedule, Cathy turns these records over to a bookkeeper, who prepares quarterly profit and loss statements. Once a year, a Certified Public Accountant prepares the company taxes and generates a full set of financial statements.

Actual payroll generation and payroll tax records are maintained by PAYCHECKS, Inc., a payroll service. Payroll is generated on the fifteenth and last day of each month.

Advisors

Martha White, CPA, prepares taxes and annual financial statements for CCSI. Ms. White is in private practice with an office located at 123 Main Street, Indianapolis. John Kennedy, a local attorney with Mayor, Jones and Smith, is CCSI's attorney. Mr. Kennedy advised CCSI to convert to a Sub-S Corporation and filed all the appropriate paperwork with the Secretary of State. Annually, Cathy meets with both Ms. White and Mr. Kennedy to review the status of the company and to discuss any updates or changes that need to be made.

Cathy has also compiled a group of four volunteers who serve as an advisory committee. Once a year, Cathy meets with these advisors to discuss her business strategies and update her business plan. Three of the four advisors are retired executives who offer their expertise based on many years of small business experience. The fourth advisor is a local businesswoman who manages a financial services business. Two of her four advisors are also CCSI customers.

Financial Information

Use of Funds

Use of loan proceeds will be as follows:

Loan Request: $1,000.00

Use of funds is for permanent working capital. A cash-flow projection follows, which demonstrates that this influx of cash will allow CCSI to service more residential and commercial customers. The cash flow outlines that the increase in sales will allow CCSI to purchase additional capital equipment beginning in the fourth month. The cash-flow projections also demonstrate an adequate ability to service the debt incurred by this loan.

The proposed loan will be secured with a first security interest in the assets of the business, as well as a personal guaranty from Cathy Smith. CCSI has no business debt at this time, and equipment with a net value (net of accumulated depreciation) of $3,500.00.

Cash-Flow Assumptions

The first assumption of the cash-flow projection is that all existing business will be retained in the next 12 months. New residential business will be in the form of one house in month 2, an additional house in month 4, a third new house in month 6, and a minor increase in rates in month 10 for a total of new residential business income of $1,680.

New commercial business consists of one new building in month 3, a second new building in month 5, and a slight increase in all commercial rates reflected in months 9-12. Total new commercial income for the year is $4,000.

The operating expenses related to new business income is reflected as 68 percent of new residential income and 69 percent of new commercial income.

This assumption is based on historical operating percentages. All fixed expenses remain the same. Loan payments begin in month 3 and are calculated at 10 percent interest for a 12-month term.

Capital equipment purchases will be made beginning in month 4 with the purchase of three new vacuum cleaners and the addition of a floor waxing unit in month 8.

Scenario 2 assumptions are basically the same as above, except that new residential and commercial sales are half the amounts stated above. Operating expenses are reduced accordingly.

Cathy's Cleaning Service, Inc.
12-Month Cash-Flow Forecast

	1	2	3	4	5	6
Beginning Cash Balance	$0	$1,110	$1,239	$1,342	$1,114	$948
Cash Inflow						
Existng Business	$2,470	$2,470	$2,470	$2,470	$2,470	$2,470
Loan Proceeds	$1,000					
Owner Contributons						
New Residental Business		$60	$60	$120	$120	$180
New Commercial Business			$200	$200	$400	$400
Total Cash Inflow	$3,470	$2,530	$2,730	$2,790	$2,990	$3,050
Cash Outflow						
Existng Operating Expenses	$1,643	$1,643	$1,643	$1,643	$1,643	$1,643
New Residental Operating Exp	$0	$41	$41	$82	$82	$122
New Commercial Operating Exp	$0	$0	$138	$138	$276	$276
Office Space	$68	$68	$68	$68	$68	$68
Utilities	$15	$15	$15	$15	$15	$15
Office Supplies	$10	$10	$10	$10	$10	$10
Business Insurance	$25	$25	$25	$25	$25	$25
Auto Expense	$50	$50	$50	$50	$50	$50
Auto Insurance	$35	$35	$35	$35	$35	$35
Pager	$14	$14	$14	$14	$14	$14
Loan Payments			$88	$88	$88	$88
Owner's Compensation	$500	$500	$500	$500	$500	$500
Capital Purchase-Vacuum Clnrs				$350	$350	$350
Capital Purchase-Floor Waxer						
Total Cash Outflow	$2,360	$2,401	$2,627	$3,018	$3,156	$3,196
Monthly change in cash	$1,110	$129	$103	($228)	($166)	($146)
Ending Cash Balance	$1,110	$1,239	$1,342	$1,114	$948	$802

Cathy's Cleaning Service _____ *Business Plan Pg. 8a*

Cathy's Cleaning Service, Inc.

12-Month Cash-Flow Forecast	7	8	9	10	I 1	12	Totals
Beginning Cash Balance	$802	$1,006	$710	$945	$1,186	$1,427	
Cash Inflow							
Existing Business	$2,470	$2,470	$2,470	$2,470	$2,470	$2,470	$29,640
Loan Proceeds							$1,000
Owner Contributions							
New Residential Business	$180	$180	$180	$200	$200	$200	$1,680
New Commercial Business	$400	$400	$500	$500	$500	$500	$4,000
Total Cash Inflow	$3,050	$3,050	$3,150	$3,170	$3,170	$3,170	$36,320
Cash Outflow							
Existing Operating Expenses	$1,643	$1,643	$1,643	$1,643	$1,643	$1,643	$19,716
New Residential Operating Exp	$122	$122	$122	$136	$136	$136	$1,142
New Commercial Operating Exp	$276	$276	$345	$345	$345	$345	$2,760
Office Space	$68	$68	$68	$68	$68	$68	$816
Utilities	$15	$15	$15	$15	$15	$15	$180
Office Supplies	$10	$10	$10	$10	$10	$10	$120
Business Insurance	$25	$25	$25	$25	$25	$25	$300
Auto Expense	$50	$50	$50	$50	$50	$50	$600
Auto Insurance	$35	$35	$35	$35	$35	$35	$420
Pager	$14	$14	$14	$14	$14	$14	$168
Loan Payments	$88	$88	$88	$88	$88	$88	$880
Owner's Compensation	$500	$500	$500	$500	$500	$500	$6,000
Capital Purchase-Vacuum Clnrs							$1,050
Capital Purchase-Floor Waxer		$500					$500
Total Cash Outflow	$2,846	$3,346	$2,915	$2,929	$2,929	$2,929	$34,652
Monthly change in cash	$204	($296)	$235	$241	$241	$241	$1,668
Ending Cash Balance	$1,006	$710	$945	$1,186	$1,427	$1,668	$1,668

Recommended Reading List

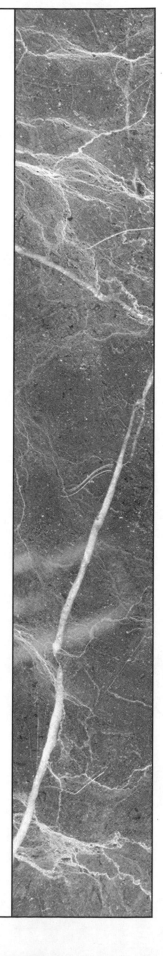

Boyett, J. *Workplace 2000: The Revolution Reshaping American Business*. New York: Dutton, 1991.

Covey, Steven. *Principle Centered Leadership*. New York: Simon & Schuster, 1992.

Covey, Steven. *The Seven Habits of Highly Effective People*. Provo: Covey Leadership Center, 1993.

Davis, S., & B. Davidson. *20/20 Vision*. New York: Simon & Schuster, 1991.

Davis, W. *Start Your Own Business for $1,000 or Less*. Dover: Upstart Publishing Company, 1995.

Deming, W. *Out of the Crisis*. Cambridge: Massachusetts Institute of Technology, Center for Advanced Engineering Study, 1986.

Edwards, P., & S. Edwards. *Best Home Businesses for the '90s: The Inside Information You Need to Know to Select a Home-Based Business That Is Right for You*. New York: G. P. Putnam & Sons, 1994.

Edwards, P., & S. Edwards. *Making It on Your Own*. New York: G. P. Putnam & Sons, 1994.

Edwards, P., & S. Edwards. *Working from Home: Everything You Need to Know About Living and Working Under the Same Roof*. New York: G. P. Putnam & Sons, 1994.

Fisher, R., & W. Ury. *Getting to Yes*. New York: Penguin Books, 1983.

Gerber, M. *E-Myth*. Cambridge: Ballinger, 1986.

Hawken, Paul. *Growing a Business*. New York: Simon & Schuster, 1987.

Kern, C. *How to Run Your Own Home Business*. Lincolnwood: VGM Career Horizons, 1995.

Kline, P. *Everyday Genius*. Arlington: Great Ocean Publishers, 1988.

McAleese, T. *Money: How to Get It, Keep It, and Make t Grow*. Ha rne: Career 1991.

McQuown, J. *Inc. Yourself*. New York: HarperBus ess, 199.

Naisbitt, J. & P. Adurdene. *Megatrends 2000*. New York: Morrow, 1990.

Parramon, J. *Lettering and Logotypes*. New York: Watson-Guptill Publications, 1991.

Ries, A., & J. Trout. *Bottom Up Marketing*. New York: McGraw-Hill, 1989.

Ries, A., & J. Trout. *Marketing Warfare*. New York: McGraw-Hill, 1991.

Stolze, W. *Start Up*. Franklin Lakes: Career Press, 1996.

Toffler, Alvin. *Powershift*. New York: Bantam Books, 1990.

Weitzen, H. *Infopreneurs*. New York: J. Wiley, 1988.